Financial Tools
for the
Non-Financial
Executive

Financial Tools
for the
Non-Financial
Executive

BRYAN E. MILLING

Chilton Book Company
Radnor, Pennsylvania

Copyright © 1983 by Bryan E. Milling
All Rights Reserved
Published in Radnor, Pennsylvania 19089,
  by Chilton Book Company

Designed by Patricia Pennington

Manufactured in the United States of America

Library of Congress Cataloging in Publication Data
Milling, Bryan E.
    Financial tools for the non-financial executive.
    Includes indexes.
    1. Corporations—Finance—Handbooks, manuals, etc.
2. Business enterprises—Finance—Handbooks, manuals,
etc. I. Title.
HG4027.3.M54   1983   658.1′5   82-70779
ISBN 0-8019-7391-0
ISBN 0-8019-7392-9 (pbk.)

1 2 3 4 5 6 7 8 9 0   2 1 0 9 8 7 6 5 4 3

Contents

Section One: Financial Management

Section Two: Performance Analysis

Section Three: Component Analysis

Section Four: Structural Analysis

Section Five: Profit-Planning and Financial Forecasting Formulas

List of Financial Facts

1. Financial management is critical to the success of every business. (Introduction, page 2)

2. Positive financial management increases earnings and reduces the risk of financial failure. (Chapter 1, page 9)

3. A balance sheet must balance. (Chapter 2, page 17)

4. Opportunity costs hurt earnings. (Chapter 3, page 25)

5. Cash flow seldom corresponds directly to financial flow. (Chapter 4, page 30)

6. Net income plus depreciation measures annual cash flow. (Chapter 4, page 35)

7. Comparative criteria provide the foundation for financial analysis. (Chapter 5, page 46)

8. Analyzing a firm's profit performance requires a look at all four views of its profit margins. (Chapter 6, page 57)

9. The ROE calculation measures the yield that a firm's earnings represent for its stockholders. (Chapter 7, page 62)

10. Return on investment provides the focal point for positive financial management. (Chapter 7, page 69)

11. The average collection period provides the best perspective for managing a firm's investment in accounts receivable. (Chapter 8, page 80)

12. Accounts receivable represent the primary source of cash for a business. (Chapter 8, page 82)

13. A change in credit terms can increase the return a business earns from its total asset investment. (Chapter 9, page 86)

14. To measure the cost of missing a cash discount, translate it into its annualized interest rate. (Chapter 9, page 91)

15. Integrated management analysis should precede any change in a firm's credit terms or policies. (Chapter 9, page 97)

16. Recognizing the days' sales a firm's stock represents provides the best perspective for inventory management. (Chapter 10, page 104)

17. A sales forecast is a necessary precedent for controlling a firm's investment in inventory. (Chapter 11, page 108)

18. The economic ordering quantity (EOQ) minimizes a firm's overall inventory costs. (Chapter 11, page 112)

19. The liquidity in a firm's financial structure enters into any estimate of its creditworthiness. (Chapter 12, page 127)

20. A business often can justify an apparent overinvestment in cash. (Chapter 12, page 129)

21. A 2:1 current ratio represents the traditional mark of an adequate level of liquidity. (Chapter 13, page 134)

22. A 1:1 quick ratio represents the traditional mark of an adequate level of liquidity. (Chapter 13, page 136)

23. Financial leverage magnifies the return on stockholders' equity (ROE) that develops from any return on assets (ROI). (Chapter 14, page 144)

24. A 2:1 debt-to-equity ratio marks the traditional limit on the financial leverage a business can safely employ. (Chapter 15, page 152)

25. Fixed operating costs magnify the gains or losses that develop from any fluctuations in sales. (Chapter 16, page 161)

26. Break-even analysis provides the foundation for profit planning in a business. (Chapter 16, page 165)

27. Financial forecasting helps anticipate a firm's financing requirements. (Chapter 17, page 174)

28. Expanding the net profit margin increases a firm's ROI. (Chapter 18, page 181)

29. Increasing the total asset turnover rate increases a firm's ROI. (Chapter 18, page 183)

30. A firm's ROE fluctuates in direct response to any change in its ROI. (Chapter 18, page 184)

Financial Tools
for the
Non-Financial
Executive

Introduction

Financial management is essential to business success, yet it is usually the last consideration for the average businessman. Instead, he concentrates on his special area of expertise—sales or engineering or manufacturing—and turns to the financial aspects of his business only when a crisis arises. Then he may become uneasy or intimidated when he has to work with the analytical tools that are essential for effective financial management. He may make decisions that influence the profitability, and perhaps the survival, of his business using information that he doesn't fully understand.

Financial Tools for the Non-Financial Executive provides a remedy for that problem. This book can be used as a formula "kit" by applying the important formulas and ratios that serve as the basic tools for financial analysis. The List of Financial Facts or index will help you locate quickly any analytic tool that you need. Since financial management requires interpretation as well as calculation, the *Formula Kit* proceeds beyond the basic arithmetic to help you understand and use the data that result from your calculations.

Is a three-to-one debt-to-equity ratio satisfactory for your business?

How does inventory turnover rate affect your financial structure?

How does your need for working capital relate to your sales volume?

As the kit helps you answer such questions, you will find that financial analysis is more than an interesting arithmetic exercise. Illustrated through

1 The Need for Financial Management

A business can survive with haphazard financial management, but rarely will it prosper, and inevitably it will forego some profits. By properly employing the principles that underlie financial management a business can increase its earnings. This chapter establishes the critical role that financial management plays in the operation of a business. That effort, or the lack of it, influences every significant aspect of a firm's operating results.

Financial analysis, the foundation for financial management, provides perspective for sensible financial management decisions. It also enables a businessman to understand his present financial circumstances and project his future prospects. Any business that ignores this fundamental analysis confronts the constant threat of financial trauma.

If you do practice *positive financial management,* you will be able to anticipate and avoid problems before they arise. Actively employing those principles can lead to higher profits.

THE FULCRUM OF FINANCIAL MANAGEMENT

Almost every business activity affects a firm's financial circumstances. For example, when a business employs trade credit to purchase inventory, it simultaneously increases both its assets and liabilities. The increase in liabilities raises the debt-to-equity ratio, creates a claim on future cash flow, firm's bottom line, the financial performance in a business cannot be gauged by earnings alone. Earnings must also be related to the stockholders' equity and to total assets. These relationships provide a measure of how efficiently a business employs the funds at its disposal. In fact, those measures should orient any financial management effort.

Whichever gauges you employ, limiting any analysis to the current year's operation still does not properly assess your financial performance. Indeed, you must compare the current year's results with those generated in previous years. Then you should compare your operating performance against that exhibited by similar firms in your industry.

POSITIVE FINANCIAL MANAGEMENT

Fundamental financial analysis is not an intellectual province reserved for sophisticated businessmen and scholars. The important concepts can be grasped easily by anyone who has some familiarity with basic accounting statements. But many businessmen often forget this and employ the principles of financial analysis only when a problem arises. A cash shortage may force a close look at an excess investment in accounts receivable; the inability to meet debt obligations promptly may encourage a look at the term structure of the firm's liabilities; or the failure to obtain increased trade credit may raise a concern about supplier payment habits. The major premise of this book is that financial management should not be a peripheral activity. Nor should it be employed only when a crisis arises. Instead, the principles of financial management should be applied consistently to contribute profitably to your firm's objectives.

Positive financial management can make a significant contribution not only to ensuring profits, but to help ensure business survival. Every business incurs risk while seeking profits. And the drive for higher profits inevitably raises the risk. The more risk a business accepts, the higher the return it can achieve. At the same time, risk represents a direct threat to business survival. The higher the level of the risk, the greater the threat. Realistically, a business should balance the risk it accepts with the profit it seeks. Too much risk relative to the potential return doesn't make financial sense.

Positive financial management recognizes the trade-off between the risk and return associated with every management decision and tries to increase earnings without incurring serious risks. These objectives are emphasized in:

FINANCIAL FACT

Positive financial management increases earnings and reduces the risk of financial failure.

Of course, objectives other than earnings are also important. Some businessmen consider a larger sales volume the most important business objective. Others seek a larger market share. Still others may consider technological advances most significant. Yet achieving any of these objectives does not ensure profitability or survival. Orienting a business primarily toward any one of those objectives can make its operations unprofitable and its survival unlikely.

2 Assessing Financial Condition

Positive financial management requires a clear view of a firm's financial circumstances and its progress. The conventional accounting reports—the balance sheet and the income statement—provide that view. This chapter reviews the basic concepts that enter into the construction of a business balance sheet, and Chapter 3 provides a similar look at the income statement.

THE BALANCE SHEET

A balance sheet lists and categorizes assets, liabilities, and owner's equity to provide an image of a firm's financial condition at a particular point, usually at the end of a month, quarter, or business year. The construction of a business balance sheet proceeds on a traditional accounting premise:

Total Assets = Total Claims Against Assets

The total assets owned by a business equal the total claims against those assets. The two totals balance.

The total claim on a firm's assets usually is divided into two categories—liabilities and stockholders' equity. Liabilities represent the primary claims on the firm's assets held by creditors. Should a business dissolve, creditors have the first right to the proceeds gained from selling the assets. The stockholders' equity represents a secondary or residual claim on assets. In the event a business ceases operations, stockholders stand behind the creditors. They are entitled only to the proceeds from the residual assets that are left after satisfying all creditor claims.

The basic accounting relationship recognizes the two categories of claims on assets:

$$Assets = Liabilities + Stockholders' Equity$$

The total assets in a business equal the total that comes from adding its liabilities to the stockholders' equity.* The two totals still balance. This fundamental accounting equation provides the foundation for the construction of a business balance sheet. For example, assume that on 12/31/82 the Sample Corporation owned $500,000 in total assets. On the same date, creditors' claims on those assets totaled $250,000; stockholders held an equal (although secondary) claim on the same assets.

The basic accounting equation presents the firm's financial image in the form of a balance sheet:

The Sample Corporation

	(12/31/82 Balance Sheet)
Total Assets	$500,000
Total Liabilities	$250,000
Stockholders' Equity	250,000
Liabilities and Equity	$500,000

Total assets still equal the total that comes from adding the liabilities to the stockholders' equity.

Unfortunately, the Sample Corporation's simple balance sheet provides little information that is useful for practical financial management. The state-

*In the place of stockholders' equity, an unincorporated enterprise typically utilizes either "owner's equity" or "proprietorship." The accounting relationship remains the same.

ment tells us nothing about the specific composition of the firm's assets. Nor does it identify the nature of its liabilities. Indeed, the corporation may be financially sound, or it may lack the capability to pay its debts promptly. Either potential exists, even though a business with equity equal to its liabilities is usually in a comfortable financial position. A realistic view of a firm's financial condition can be obtained only by categorizing assets and liabilities.

On the left side of the equation, a firm's assets are separated into one of two categories. One category includes all *current* assets. The other contains *fixed* assets. The major current assets usually include all of a firm's cash, accounts receivable, and inventory. Current assets continuously *revolve* through the firm. Thus a business employs cash to purchase inventory, often using trade credit to defer payment. In some circumstances, sales convert inventory directly back into cash. Then the process repeats itself.

Since most business sales are made in exchange for accounts receivable, a business has to wait ten to thirty days or longer for the actual cash payment for each customer's purchase. Whatever the circumstance, current assets normally revolve through a business several times during a year. The cash to inventory to accounts receivable to cash transition constantly repeats itself.

In contrast, the building, machinery, and equipment owned by a business are fixed assets, since they represent a relatively permanent investment necessary to carry on operations. Fixed assets also revolve. More efficient machinery and equipment replace that made obsolete by age or new technology. But fixed assets typically revolve slowly through a business. So, at any time, the assets can be considered permanent.

The comparative *liquidity* exhibited by the two categories of assets is the distinguishing factor. Liquidity provides a relative measure of how easily a business can convert an asset into the cash necesary to meet its obligations. The easier the conversion, the more liquid the asset.

Current assets typically demonstrate a high degree of liquidity. Of course, cash itself sets the standard. The more cash it holds, the more able a business will be to meet its obligations promptly.

Accounts receivable usually come next on the scale of relative liquidity. Collections continuously convert a portion of a firm's receivables into cash. The typical business collects all of its existing receivables every thirty to forty-five days.

Inventory is the least liquid current asset because a business must generate a sale to convert any inventory into cash. If the sale is made in exchange for an account receivable, the business receives no cash until the customer fulfills his promise to pay. Nevertheless, an aggressive sales effort still can convert inventory into cash in a relatively short period.

In contrast, fixed assets exhibit almost no liquidity. From one perspective, they are necessary for a firm's operations. Selling the assets to generate cash isn't a realistic consideration. From another perspective, a business usually finds it difficult to sell any fixed assets at a fair price within a reasonable time. Indeed, fixed assets represent a permanent investment, not a source of funds to pay creditors.

To emphasize the distinction between current assets and fixed assets, let's take a closer look at the $500,000 in total assets owned by the Sample Corporation at 12/31/82:

The Sample Corporation

	(12/31/82 Balance Sheet)	
Cash	$ 50,000	
Accounts Receivable	175,000	
Inventory	150,000	
Total Current Assets		$375,000
Factory Building	$ 75,000	
Machinery and Equipment	50,000	
Total Fixed Assets		$125,000
Total Assets		$500,000

The Sample Corporation has $375,000 in liquid assets that it probably can convert into cash within a relatively short period. Completely converting all current assets into cash becomes necessary only when a business ceases operations. Nevertheless, creditors (and stockholders) usually view all of the current assets in a business as a potential source of funds to retire its existing liabilities.

The corporation also has $125,000 in fixed assets. Those assets—a small factory building, machinery, and equipment—represent the permanent investment necessary for the firm's operations. The cash value held in those assets may be more or less than the accounting value included on the balance sheet. However, any difference in valuation is relatively unimportant since the Sample Corporation needs the assets to continue operations. No business voluntarily sells its fixed assets to pay creditors.*

On the other side of the accounting equation, liabilities also are separated into two categories. One category contains current, or short-term, liabilities; the other includes deferred, or long-term, liabilities.

Current liabilities include all obligations payable within one year or less. Those obligations usually have a close relationship to a firm's current assets. Thus accounts payable to trade creditors for inventory purchases represent current liabilities normally due within thirty days or less. Short-term loans from banks or other lenders also represent current liabilities. Such loans typically supplement supplier trade credit and help support the borrower's investment in current assets. Similarly, the business repays such loans from the cash gained from liquidating a portion of those assets.

Deferred, or long-term, liabilities represent obligations that will not come due within the year following the date of the balance sheet. The business temporarily defers repayment of those obligations. Businesses can incur liabilities that require repayment on a monthly schedule that covers a number of years, but all payments due in the upcoming year qualify as current liabilities. The rest of the obligation remains a long-term liability.

The Sample Corporation's balance sheet illustrates the distinction between current and deferred liabilities.

On 12/31/82 creditors held $175,000 in current claims on the Sample Corporation's assets. The firm has to generate the funds necessary to satisfy those obligations during 1983 or risk financial embarrassment. At the same time, it can defer any immediate action on the $75,000 in long-term liabilities. None of those liabilities comes due before 1984. Of course, the $175,000 in current liabilities are not all immediately due and payable. But look at the $100,000 in accounts payable. Chances are that those obligations come due in the first thirty days of the year.

Accounts payable usually revolve in the same way as current assets do. The business retires accounts payable as they fall due on a day-to-day basis. Then it makes purchases that create new payables. Of course, accounts payable revolve only so long as the business pays the maturing obligations on time. Suppliers soon stop selling to the business that falls too far past due.

The Sample Corporation also has a $50,000 note payable classified as a current liability. The note presumably represents a bank loan that helps support the current assets. While the liability is current, payment may not

---

*A sale and lease-back arrangement is one prominent exception.

The Sample Corporation

	(12/31/82 Balance Sheet)
Accounts Payable $100,000	
Note Payable 50,000	
Other Current Liabilities 25,000	
Total Current Liabilities	$175,000
Long-Term Liabilities	75,000
Total Liabilities	$250,000
Capital Stock $100,000	
Retained Earnings 150,000	
Total Stockholders' Equity	$250,000
Equity and Liabilities	$500,000

be required until several months into the year. Moreover, such loans commonly are renewed or rolled over. So the note draws less immediate attention than the Sample Corporation's accounts payable.

Drawing even less attention are those obligations lumped together as "other current liabilities." Such obligations usually include the current portion of a firm's deferred debt, as well as short-term, recurring liabilities accrued in the normal course of business. We can assume that the Sample Corporation's 12/31/82 balance sheet properly recognizes accrued payroll, taxes, or interest expenses among the other current liabilities.

This slice from the Sample Corporation's balance sheet also categorizes the basic elements that make up the stockholder's claims on assets. The $100,000 in capital stock represents the stockholders' actual cash investment in the firm. In addition, earnings retained in the business since inception—that is, those not paid out as dividends—total $150,000. Although left in the business, those earnings represent an increase in the accounting value of each share of stock held by an investor.

Categorizing the asset, liability, and stockholders' equity accounts still doesn't provide a complete picture of a firm's financial position. That picture appears only when those accounts are combined into the traditional balance-sheet format. The Sample Corporation's balance sheet in Table 2–1 enables us to interrelate these elements, and the nature of those interrelationships raises some critical questions for the financial manager.

Table 2-1. Financial Condition of the Sample Corporation

	(12/31/82 Balance Sheet)	
Cash	$ 50,000	
Accounts Receivable	175,000	
Inventory	150,000	
Total Current Assets		$375,000
Factory Building	$ 75,000	
Machinery and Equipment	50,000	
Total Fixed Assets		$125,000
Total Assets		$500,000
Accounts Payable	$100,000	
Note Payable	50,000	
Other Current Liabilities	25,000	
Total Current Liabilities		$175,000
Long-Term Liabilities		75,000
Total Liabilities		$250,000
Common Stock	$100,000	
Retained Earnings	150,000	
Total Stockholders' Equity		$250,000
Total Liabilities and Equity		$500,000

What is the relationship between the firm's debt and equity? Is either one too large relative to the other? Remember that too much debt relative to equity threatens the firm's survival. Too much equity relative to debt reduces the return on the stockholders' investment. What is the relationship between current assets and current liabilities? Current assets provide the funds necessary to meet current liabilities as they come due.

Even when a business has a comfortable cushion of total current assets relative to its total current liabilities, it still may not escape financial problems, particularly when inventory and accounts receivable make up most of the current assets. A business can't pay an expense or retire a liability with either asset. Instead, it needs *cash* to meet its obligations, and even a profitable business can find itself short of that critical asset.

Employing the analytic tools demonstrated throughout the book would indicate that the Sample Corporation is financially sound. The fundamental relationships apparent in the firm's financial image fall within the guidelines that define prudent financial management.

THE IMPORTANCE OF BALANCED ACCOUNTS

One of the most important basic accounting tenets is that a balance sheet must balance. A change in any asset, liability, or equity account effects a comparable change in other accounts that make up the balance sheet. No account can change independently. For example, the decision to increase inventory requires a matching change elsewhere in a firm's financial structure. In some circumstances, a business will exchange cash for the inventory. One asset replaces another.

Often an increase in liabilities accompanies the initial increase in a firm's assets. The business employs trade credit—accounts payable or other borrowed funds—to finance the asset acquisition. Less frequently, an increase in stockholders' equity will provide the funds necessary to increase assets.

In any event, no balance-sheet account can change without a corresponding change in another balance-sheet account. Overlooking this relationship in the midst of all of the daily management decisions necessary to operate a business can lead to some serious financial problems. That potential justifies recognition of that important accounting principle in:

FINANCIAL FACT

A balance sheet
must balance.

The total assets owned by a business must equal the total claims on those assets. Almost every business decision affects that relationship. Consequently, that relationship should become a consideration in almost every business decision.

3 The Measure of Financial Progress

A balance sheet projects an image of a firm's financial condition at a particular point. The most recent balance sheet actually summarizes the cumulative results of all of a firm's financial transactions since it initiated operations, but it provides little information about recent financial progress. Consequently, a well-managed business complements any analysis of the balance sheet with a review of the income statement.

An income statement measures the financial gain or loss generated by a business *between* two points, such as from the beginning to the end of a month, quarter, or year. The prudent financial manager measures the firm's gains or losses across all of those periods.

THE BOTTOM LINE

An income statement matches the expenses incurred by a business during a specific period against its sales. The difference between the two measures the operating results for that period. For example, assume that the Sample Corporation generates $1 million in sales and incurs $950,000 in expenses for the twelve months ending 12/31/82. A simplified income statement measures the firm's operating results as:

Sales	$1,000,000
Expenses	(950,000)
Net Income	$ 50,000

The bottom line of the income statement—the central concern for most businessmen—isolates the Sample Corporation's $50,000 in profits for the year ending 12/31/82. That translates directly into a $50,000 increase in the stockholders' equity account on the firm's balance sheet. Of course, this simplified income statement provides little information that is useful for positive financial management. A more practical statement for management analysis and action *categorizes* a firm's expenses.

Expense Categories

A properly constructed income statement organizes the total expenses a business incurs during an operating period into three major categories:

1. Cost of goods sold
2. Operating expenses
3. Interest expenses

The cost-of-goods-sold total represents all of the expenses associated with the inventory actually sold during an operating period, including material purchase costs. However, a manufacturer would add in the labor and overhead expenses incurred in the production process.

It is important to note that the cost of goods sold by a business seldom coincides with the cost of inventories purchased or produced during an operating period. Nor does that total match the cost of inventory on hand at the beginning or the end of the period covered by an income statement. But an important interrelationship does exist between the cost-of-goods-sold total and the inventory on hand at the beginning—that purchased (or manufactured)—and that on hand at the end of an operating period:

> Beginning Inventory
> Plus: *Additions to Inventory*
> Equals: Total Inventory Available for Sale
> Minus: *Ending Inventory*
> Equals: Cost of Goods Sold

The total goods available for sale during an operating period include a firm's beginning inventory plus all additions made to inventory during the period. Subtracting the inventory on hand at the end of the operating period from that total identifies the cost of goods sold.

Most expenses, apart from those associated with the acquisition or manufacture of inventory, fit into the operating-expense category. These include the expenses that arise from marketing the firm's products, as well as the general and administrative expenses associated with operating a business. However, a unique characteristic makes interest expenses a separate category on an income statement. These expenses arise from the financial structure of the firm rather than directly from its operations. Even though interest expenses can significantly affect the bottom line in a business, they stand apart from operating expenses. A financial structure without debt eliminates interest expenses, but a business always incurs operating expenses.

One cost incurred by a successful business does not fit into any of the three major expense categories. That is the income tax assessed against the firm's earnings. Since it doesn't qualify as an operational or financial expense, it appears on an income statement as a separate deduction. Although income taxes are significant in a profitable business, they stand apart from actual operating expenses.

Let's see how the major expense categories enter into the final construction of an income statement.

Reaching the Bottom Line

The bottom line of an income statement registers a firm's operating results, measuring the difference between total revenues and total expenses. However, simply comparing those two totals provides little useful information for positive financial management. Consequently, before reaching the bottom line, an income statement subtracts each category of expenses in turn from the total sales revenue. The amount remaining after each deduction provides a different perspective of a firm's operating results. The view at each step helps isolate the factors that determine earnings.

Let's expand the Sample Corporation's income statement for the year ending 12/31/82 to illustrate the financial views that develop as an income statement progresses from a firm's sales to its bottom line. That illustration begins by dividing the $950,000 in total costs incurred during that year into the appropriate categories:

1. Cost of Goods Sold...................................	$700,000
2. Operating Expenses	205,000
3. Interest Expenses	20,000
4. Taxes	25,000
Total Expenses	$950,000

Beginning with the Sample Corporation's $1,000,000 sales volume for the year ending 12/31/82, the income statement first subtracted the cost of goods sold to measure the firm's *gross profit:*

Sales	$1,000,000
Cost of Goods Sold	(700,000)
Gross Profit..	$ 300,000

The gross profit indicates the actual gains that proceed from sales. These gains represent the total margin available to cover operating expenses, as well as to provide any earnings the business might enjoy.

The income statement then subtracts the total operating expenses from gross profit. This identifies the firm's *operating income.* Some statements refer to that total as the *earnings before interest and taxes,* or EBIT. In the Sample Corporation's circumstance:

Gross Profit	$300,000
Operating Expenses	(205,000)
Operating Income (or EBIT)	$ 95,000

Operating income represents the *pure profits* generated by a business. The profits are pure in the sense that they ignore financing costs and income-tax assessments not directly related to operations. Relating those pure profits to total sales provides another important measure of a firm's operating efficiency.

The income statment then deducts any interest charges incurred from operating income. That measures the firm's *earnings before taxes,* or EBT. The Sample Corporation's income statement continues:

Operating Income	$95,000
Interest Charges	(20,000)
Earnings Before Taxes (EBT)	$75,000

The earnings-before-taxes total recognizes the effects of a firm's financial structure on its operating results. The larger the debt load, the more significant the effect. That should not imply that a business should avoid using debt, but any debt employed should contribute to an increase in operating income that exceeds its interest cost.

From another perspective, the earnings-before-taxes total provides an important indication of a firm's ability to absorb a financial setback. Any drop in gross profit or increase in expenses must exceed the earnings-before-taxes total in order to impose a loss on a business. Naturally, that presumes that the firm's past earnings level will continue at the same rate in the future.

To complete the progression from the total sales to the bottom line, an income statement recognizes a firm's income-tax obligation. That assessment does not qualify as a business expense, since it contributes nothing to a firm's operations. Nevertheless, it does reduce the net earnings retained by a business. The income statement subtracts that obligation from the earnings before taxes to identify the firm's *net income.* Completing the Sample Corporation's income statement:

Earnings Before Taxes	$75,000
Income Taxes	(25,000)
Net Income	$50,000

Net income represents the most important measure of a firm's operating results. Indeed, the bottom line stands as the final symbol of business success or failure.

But the financial manager must look beyond the bottom line because the net income actually represents a *residual*—what's left over from all the financial interrelationships associated with operating a business. Table 3–1 emphasizes their significance with the view of the Sample Corporation's complete income statement. That view emphasizes the major factors that determine the bottom-line results.

Incidentally, the distinction between a firm's before and after tax income does not affect the principles that orient most financial management decisions. Thus most of the discussion that follows recognizes a firm's potential income-tax obligations only when they enter into an actual decision process.

One major qualification should be added to the information apparent in a business income statement: It summarizes only the visible financial factors that determine a firm's net income. The financial manager also must recognize another perspective of business income—opportunity costs.

Table 3-1. The Sample Corporation Income Statement

	(Year Ending 12/31/82)
Sales	$1,000,000
Cost of Goods Sold	700,000
Gross Profit	$ 300,000
Operating Expenses	205,000
Operating Income (EBIT)	95,000
Interest Charges	20,000
Earnings Before Taxes (EBT)	$ 75,000
Taxes	25,000
Net Income	$ 50,000

OPPORTUNITY COSTS

The bottom line of an income statement registers the actual profits generated by a business. In any circumstance, profits represent financial progress and increase the stockholders' equity. However, to set the stage for later discussion, a distinction should be drawn between the earnings recognized by an income statement and a firm's actual financial performance. Standing alone, the net profit that appears on an income statement does not adequately measure financial performance. Any *opportunity costs* incurred must also be recognized.

In simple terms, opportunity costs represent profits foregone. The firm that incurs opportunity costs not only fails to realize its full earnings potential, but it earns less than it should. Indeed, a satisfactory performance measured in terms of actual profits may become less so in light of opportunity costs.

In some instances, opportunity costs can be measured directly. Thus a business incurs an opportunity cost when it fails to take trade discounts offered by its suppliers. Each discount lost represents earnings foregone. For example, assume that a business buys $200,000 in material during the year from suppliers who allow a 2% discount for payment within ten days after each purchase. Should the business fail to take those discounts, it incurs $4,000 in opportunity costs ($200,000 × 2%). The lost earnings can be measured directly.

Many opportunity costs incurred by a business are more elusive, subject only to indirect measurement or management estimates. For example, a business incurs an opportunity cost whenever it lacks the stock necessary to fill a customer's order. If the customer accepts later delivery, the firm's opportunity cost—the stock-out cost—is limited to the administrative expense associated with a back order. However, if the customer decides to buy from a competitor, the opportunity cost becomes the potential profit on the lost sale. If the inconvenience makes the customer shift all of his future purchases to competitors, the opportunity cost then becomes the potential profits on all of those lost sales. Stock-out costs do not appear in an income statement, but they still damage the firm's earnings.

A business also incurs opportunity costs when it holds assets in excess of the minimum necessary for its operations. Should the business have to employ borrowed funds to carry those assets, the opportunity costs appear in the form of higher interest expenses on the income statement. Eliminating the excess assets and associated interest costs can increase the firm's earnings.

Even in the absence of any debt, excess assets impose another, less apparent opportunity cost: the income foregone on the funds invested in the excess assets. Thus dollars invested in excess accounts receivable might increase the firm's earnings if used to buy additional inventory. Alternatively, dollars invested in excess inventory might be profitably employed in fixed assets that will improve a firm's operating efficiency. From the most conservative viewpoint, eliminating any excess assets frees funds for investment in interest-bearing instruments that contribute to earnings.

The *Formula Kit* shows why effective control of the investment in assets should be a focal point for positive financial management. Here we only suggest that excess assets impose another opportunity cost on a business, either directly or indirectly. The financial damage that can result from that can be emphasized in:

FINANCIAL FACT

Opportunity costs
hurt earnings.

Opportunity costs do not appear as a separate expense category on the income statement, but they are nonetheless real. Chapter 4 discusses the important distinction between the financial progress measured by an income statement and the actual cash flow in a business.

bursements necessary to pay those expenses rose more rapidly than the cash collections that proceeded from the sales increase. The profitable growth spurt exhausted Beta's cash operating balance. What happened?

THE CASH VIEW

The cash flow problem that accompanied Beta's sales increase developed inevitably from the pattern apparent in the firm's collection, purchase, and payment habits:

1. Beta collects 70% of the accounts receivable arising from each month's sales in the month immediately following; the payments for the remaining 30% of each month's volume comes in the second month following the sales.
2. Beta accurately anticipates each month's sales volume and purchases only the inventory necessary for that volume.
3. Beta respects the thirty-day trade credit terms suppliers allow for all purchases; consequently, cash payment for purchases actually occurs in the same month that Beta sells the inventory.
4. Beta pays all operating expenses in the same month incurred.

The cash flow that developed from Beta's collection and disbursement history was adequate for Beta's monthly $100,000 volume during 1982. At that volume, monthly cash collections matched monthly cash expenditures. Beta's $20,000 operating cash balance absorbed any temporary disruptions in the normal cash flow pattern.

The cash requirements set by Beta's rising sales volume in February and March quickly absorbed that $20,000 operating balance and forced the business into a deficit cash position. Table 4–1 illustrates the cash accounting process that traces the natural development of that problem. The table summarizes the Beta Company's actual cash receipts and expenditures for the first three months of 1983.

January's cash flow continues the convenient balance between receipts and expenditures set by the firm's break-even operations during 1982. Cash collections from November and December sales match the $100,000 in cash expenditures necessary to conduct January's business. Beta begins and ends the month with the same $20,000 cash balance.

The sales spurt in February upsets that balance. Beta begins that month

Table 4-1. Beta Company, Cash Receipts and Expenditures

	January	February	March
Beginning cash	$ 20,000	$ 20,000	$ 2,500
Collections:			
70% of Prior* Month's Sales	70,000	70,000	87,500
30% of Second* Month's Sales	30,000	30,000	30,000
Total Cash Available	$120,000	$120,000	$120,000
Disbursements:			
Purchases	$ 70,000	$87,500	$105,000
Operating Expenses	30,000	30,000	30,000
Ending Cash	$ 20,000	$ 2,500	($ 15,000)

*Assumes that Beta's monthly sales volume totaled $100,000 in both November and December of 1982.

with the same $20,000 balance left at the end of January. The firm then collects $100,000 in payments for sales generated during the previous two months. However, the cash payments necessary for February's larger sales volume total $117,500. The $17,500 increase in expenditures comes from the higher costs necessary to generate that volume. Beta then ends February with only $2,500 in cash on hand, which becomes the beginning cash balance in March. It then collects $117,500 from sales made in January and February. Those collections plus the beginning balance provide the firm with $120,000 to meet March's cash expenditure requirements.

Unfortunately, Beta's March cash expenditure requirements total $135,000. The firm needs $105,000 to pay the inventory purchase costs that enter into that month's cost of goods sold, plus $30,000 to pay normal operating expenses. Those requirements leave Beta $15,000 short of the cash necessary to fund its operations in March. Indeed, as shown in Table 4–1, the firm presumably ends March with a $15,000 cash deficit. No business can conduct operations with a real cash deficit, so Beta filled the gap in its cash flow by temporarily deferring payment to some suppliers. That damaged the firm's credit rating, but it avoided the financial embarrassment that comes from bouncing checks.

The important principle illustrated by Beta's experience is that the financial flow that develops from the accrual accounting process seldom corresponds directly to the actual cash flow. Beta accrued $22,500 in profits during the first quarter of 1982, but it ended March with a $15,000 cash deficit. Add on the $20,000 in cash on hand at the beginning of the year and Beta's deficit cash flow during the first quarter actually totals $35,000. The potential for cash deficits makes the distinction between the financial and cash flows in a business essential:

FINANCIAL FACT

Cash flow seldom
corresponds directly
to financial flow.

Cash flow and financial flow are closely interrelated. Collections translate sales accrued as accounts receivable into cash. Similarly, cash retires the accounts payable that accrue from purchases made with trade credit. Every accrual accounting entry registers or anticipates a cash receipt or disbursement, but seldom do they all occur simultaneously.

PROFITS VERSUS CASH FLOW

Another view of the Beta Company's circumstances helps clarify the distinction between accrued profits and cash flow. The balance sheets in Table 4–2 provide a comparative view of Beta's financial position at 12/31/82 and 3/31/83.

The financial image on the 12/31/82 balance sheet developed from Beta's $100,000 monthly break-even sales volume. Previously noted was the firm's $20,000 operating cash balance. The $130,000 in accounts receivable includes $100,000 from December sales plus $30,000 still outstanding from November sales. The $70,000 inventory provides the stock necessary to satisfy January's sales volume.

In the liability section of the 12/31/82 balance sheet is the $70,000 in

Table 4-2. Beta Company, Comparative Balance Sheets

	12/31/82	3/31/83
Cash	$ 20,000	($ 15,000)
Accounts Receivable	130,000	187,500
Inventory	70,000	105,000
Total Assets	$220,000	$277,500
Accounts Payable	$ 70,000	$105,000
Bank Loan	50,000	50,000
Total Liabilities	$120,000	$155,000
Common Stock	$ 50,000	$ 50,000
Retained Earnings	50,000	72,500
Total Liabilities and Equity	$220,000	$277,500

accounts payable for the inventory purchased during December. Beta's creditors allow thirty days trade credit for purchases. So the cash payment for all of December's purchases comes due in January. Beta also has a $50,000 bank loan.

Finally, the stockholders' equity account at 12/31/82 totals $100,000. Half of that amount represents the stockholders' original investment. The other half accrued from earnings generated prior to 1982. The $100,000 total equity leaves Beta in reasonably sound financial shape. Coupled with Beta's liabilities, the equity provides the funds adequate for the level of operations that prevailed throughout 1982. However, the 3/31/83 blance sheet demonstrates how Beta's profitable sales increase upset that relationship.

Note the $22,500 increase in retained earnings on the 3/31/83 balance sheet. This corresponds with Beta's first-quarter earnings. Each dollar in profit naturally increases the stockholders' equity account by a comparable amount. But that financial progress did not prevent Beta's $15,000 cash deficit at 3/31/83. In fact, the higher sales volume actually caused the problem. The deficit developed from the expansion in accounts receivable and inventory that proceeded naturally from the sales increase.

Thus Beta's accounts receivable at 3/31/83 totaled $187,500, which represents $150,000 created from March's sales, plus 30% (or $37,500) still uncollected from February's sales. More significantly, it represents a $57,500 increase over the total outstanding at 12/31/82. The firm's inventory also increased from $70,000 at 12/31/82 to $105,000 at 3/31/83. Beta anticipated another $150,000 sales volume in April 1983.

As Financial Fact 3 reminds us, a balance sheet must balance. The $92,500 incremental investment in accounts receivable and inventory cannot accrue independently. Those funds must flow from sources that register a corresponding cumulative change in Beta's other balance sheet accounts.

Another look at Table 4–2 indicates that a portion of the necessary funds came from a $35,000 increase in accounts payable from 12/31/82 to 3/31/83.* That complements the increase in inventory necessary to accommodate April's projected $150,000 sales volume. Beta's $22,500 increase in retained earnings also helps balance the increase in receivables and inventory. However, since the firm's bank loan remained constant, that exhausted the source of funds available from the bottom side of the balance sheet.

Beta's cash account provided the only other source for the remaining $35,000 necessary to match the increase in receivables and inventory. That absorbed the $20,000 operating balance held at 12/31/82 and left the firm with a $15,000 cash deficit. Of course, presuming that Beta continues the profitable $150,000 monthly sales volume, the hypothetical deficit will soon disappear. Profits originally accrued as a portion of a firm's receivables become cash when collected. But this should not obscure the point that accounting profits do not necessarily provide immediate cash benefits for a business. The businessman who overlooks this may find his profitable operation running out of cash.

The Need for Both Views

The accrual accounting process employed to construct an income statement is essential for financial management. The process operates on the premise that a business should recognize a sale when it occurs, regardless of when it receives cash payment for the sale. Accrual accounting also registers expenses as incurred, regardless of when the business actually remits payment. Properly matching sales and expenses is the only way to assess financial performance during any particular operating period.

The accrual accounting process also underlies the construction of a business balance sheet. Properly accruing, matching, and categorizing as-

---

*To help emphasize the point of the illustration, we disregard the deferred payments to suppliers that temporarily solved Beta's cash flow problem.

sets, liabilities, and equity is the only way to evaluate a firm's financial position.

The Beta Company's experience clearly illustrates that a financial manager also needs a clear perception of the cash flow process, since he must anticipate the firm's required cash disbursements and project its cash receipts. Then he must fill any void that develops when the required cash disbursements outpace the cash receipts. The failure to maintain the distinction between accrued sales or income and current cash receipts can lead to financial embarrassment.

ANNUAL CASH FLOW

The bottom line of an income statement provides the first estimate of a firm's financial progress. The second estimate adds any depreciation expenses to the earnings total to measure annual cash flow. This total identifies the net incremental cash generated from the firm's operations. The financial manager views the annual cash flow as funds available to retire debt, pay dividends, or increase assets.

The annual cash flow generated seldom appears as a clearly delineated increase in a firm's bank account because it is usually lost in the daily fluctuations in cash receipts and disbursements. In fact, many businessmen find the concept itself somewhat questionable. While it is easy to accept income as a source of cash, it is more difficult to see how depreciation contributes to annual cash flow.

A look at the Common Company, a young service company, clarifies the concept. Common initiated operations with $150,000 in cash invested by its stockholders. The company employed $100,000 to purchase the equipment necessary for its operations. That left $50,000 as an operating cash balance:

Cash		$ 50,000
Equipment (cost)	$100,000	
Less: Accumulated Depreciation	—	
Equipment (net)		100,000
Total Assets		$150,000
Stockholders' Equity		$150,000

During its first year in business, the Common Company generated $50,000 in earnings from $500,000 in sales. The firm's $450,000 in total expenses that year included $20,000 in depreciation. That reflected management's decision to employ straight-line depreciation for the five-year useful life anticipated from Common's equipment. Straight-line depreciation takes the depreciable cost of an asset and divides it by its useful life to determine the annual depreciation expense.

Common's management also made an important decision before initiating operations: to conduct business during the first year strictly on a cash basis. The firm paid cash for all purchases and operating expenses and received cash for all sales:

Cash Sales	$500,000
Cash Expenses	(430,000)
Depreciation	(20,000)
Net Income	$ 50,000

The income statement emphasizes that depreciation is a *noncash* expense for the Common Company. The firm paid cash for its equipment at the time purchased, but that actually represented an exchange of assets— $100,000 in cash for $100,000 in equipment. Subsequently, the depreciation expense that allocates the cost of the equipment over its life requires no cash outlay. So coupling that expense with income actually measures Common's annual cash flow from operations. Depreciation represents a source of cash for the business.

To prove that claim, look at Common's balance sheet at the end of its first year in business:

Cash		$120,000
Equipment (cost)	$100,000	
Less: Accumulated Depreciation	(20,000)	
Equipment (net)		80,000
Total Assets		$200,000
Stockholders' Equity		$200,000

The $50,000 increase in the stockholders' equity account over the stockholders' initial investment matches Common's $50,000 in earnings for the year. At the same time, the net value of the firm's equipment ($80,000) reflects the $20,000 depreciation charge against the historical cost.

Finally, observe the sources of the $120,000 held in Common's cash account at the end of its first year:

Cash from Original Investment	$ 50,000
Cash from Net Income	50,000
Cash from Depreciation	20,000
Cash per Balance Sheet	$120,000

Common's $20,000 noncash depreciation expense translates directly into a $20,000 increase in the firm's cash balance. In any circumstance, coupling that expense with net income measures the annual cash flow generated by a business. This view of the firm's cash flow can be emphasized in:

FINANCIAL FACT

6

Net income plus
depreciation measures
annual cash flow.

5 The Foundation for Financial Analysis

The balance sheet and income statement are the raw material for financial management. However, the information from them must be distilled before a firm's financial position can be evaluated and its financial performance assessed. The distilling process—financial analysis—uses a number of ratios and formulas to extract and interrelate the elements included in financial statements in order to identify a firm's strengths and weaknesses. This chapter reviews the management logic and criteria that provide the foundation for effective financial analysis.

A SAMPLE ANALYSIS

Another look at the Sample Corporation, focusing on the interrelationship between the firm's investment in inventory and its average sales volume, demonstrates how financial analysis can help increase earnings. Specifically, information from Sample's balance sheet (Table 2–1) and income statement (Table 3–1) help to identify the average age of the firm's inventory. But how can the Sample Corporation use that information profitably?

The average age of the inventory owned by a business tells us how many days a typical item remains in stock before being sold. A two-step calculation identifies that average:

1. Divide a firm's annual cost of goods sold by 360 to obtain the average daily cost of goods sold
2. Divide the firm's current investment in inventory by the average daily cost-of-goods-sold total

Table 3–1 shows that the Sample Corporation's cost of goods sold totaled $700,000 for the year ending 12/31/82. So the first calculation becomes:

$$\frac{\text{Average Daily}}{\text{Cost of Goods Sold}} = \frac{\$700,000}{360} = \$1,944$$

From Table 2–1, Sample's inventory at 12/31/82 totaled $150,000. To complete the calculation:

$$\text{Average Age of Inventory} = \frac{\$150,000}{\$\ 1,944} = 77 \text{ days}$$

At 12/31/82 the average inventory item remained in the Sample Corporation's stock for seventy-seven days. From another perspective, we can say that the company has inventory on hand to meet its normal sales requirements for that period.

To recognize how the Sample Corporation can use that information to increase its earnings requires a look at the $50,000 bank note that appears on the 12/31/82 balance sheet. Previously, we surmised that those borrowed funds helped support Sample's investment in current assets. Here we will look at the $8,000 in interest the business paid on the note during 1982.

The basic accounting equation indicates that reducing the Sample Corporation's assets will eliminate the need for the support provided by the bank loan. The seventy-seven-day average inventory age suggests one potential approach.

Assume that most of the Sample Corporation's suppliers fill every order from the company within thirty days. In no circumstance does the company have to wait more than forty-five days for delivery. Certainly a business with such dependable suppliers does not need inventory on hand sufficient for seventy-seven days' sales, so at 12/31/82 the Sample Corporation is overstocked.

The firm can eliminate the overstock by deferring unnecessary purchases, thus reducing the average age of its inventory from seventy-seven to perhaps fifty days. Each day's reduction in the average age lowers the firm's inventory by $1,944. That simultaneously reduces the need for the bank loan by an equal amount.

The full twenty-seven-day reduction in the average age of the Sample Corporation's inventory reduces the firm's total assets by $52,488 ($1,944 × 27). That eliminates the need for the $50,000 bank loan as well as the $8,000 interest expense. At the same time, inventory sufficient for fifty days' sales leaves the Sample Corporation with a comfortable cushion against unforeseen delays in supplier deliveries. The firm has little risk of sustaining any stock-out costs.

The management perspective gained from a simple, two-step calculation process opens the door to higher profits for the Sample Corporation. But a *complete* analysis of the firm's financial circumstances might provide even more profitable opportunities.

METHOD AND MEANING

The Sample Corporation's experience demonstrates the profit potential of financial analysis and illustrates the important distinction between *calculation* and *interpretation*—the difference between method and meaning.

Ratios and formulas can be used to summarize and quantify financial interrelationships. But no management magic rests on a financial ratio, nor does a financial formula conjure up any management sorcery. The results of any calculation merely provide another view of a firm's financial circumstances. And that view becomes meaningful for management only when set within the context of a firm's unique circumstances.

Thus for the Sample Corporation, the seventy-seven-day average age for inventory initially stands only as an isolated financial fact—how long the average inventory item remains in stock. This fact stands out only when we recognize the efficient service provided by the firm's suppliers, which made the profitable reduction in inventory feasible.

Alternatively, a business subject to erratic supplier shipping practices might find a seventy-seven-day average inventory age necessary to provide an adequate safety stock.* Or a unique marketing strategy or an anticipated boost in sales might encourage a business to carry more inventory than necessary when measured by normal standards. So financial ratios and formulas are used to initiate financial analysis, but management must supply the meaning that makes that analysis useful.

* Safety stock represents that portion of a firm's inventory designed to help reduce or prevent stock-out costs.

ANALYTIC CRITERIA

Common sense is an essential ingredient in financial analysis, but using some comparative analytic criteria significantly increases the benefits that develop from that management attribute. Many ratios are meaningful only when placed against a benchmark or standard for comparison. Those benchmarks are obtained from three sources:

1. Traditional criteria
2. Industry criteria
3. Internal criteria.

Traditional Comparative Criteria

Traditional rules of thumb provide a number of comparative financial management standards. For example, a two-to-one debt-to-equity ratio—a firm's total debt divided by its total equity—traditionally marks the maximum credit limit for a business. Creditors supply two dollars to that business for every dollar supplied by the owners. A higher ratio presumably makes a business financially unstable. The creditors' risk of not being repaid becomes too high. To avoid that risk, many refuse to extend additional credit to a firm with a debt/equity ratio that exceeds the traditional two-to-one standard.

A two-to-one *current* ratio is another traditional mark of financial stability. That ratio—total current assets divided by total current liabilities—presumably provides a firm with the liquidity necessary to withstand an unforeseen business setback. As the current ratio falls below two-to-one, so does a firm's ability to absorb a financial reverse.

Of course, many financially sound businesses have debt/equity ratios that exceed the two-to-one traditional standard, whereas others function comfortably with current ratios of less than two-to-one. But the standard ratio provides a benchmark for comparison.

Industry Comparative Criteria

The most sensible approach to informative financial analysis focuses on comparative ratios obtained from other firms in the same industry. This comparison provides valuable insight into the relative financial condition and performance of a firm. For example, a firm's two-to-one debt/equity ratio satisfies the traditional guideline, but if the ratio is well above the industry standard, the business may be operating at a disadvantage relative to its competitors. A significant difference suggests the need for further investigation.

Any comparative analysis should employ data from companies with *similar* operating characteristics. It makes little sense to compare a local firm with a $1 million annual sales volume to a national one generating $100 million in sales annually. Financial guidelines appropriate for one probably are ill-suited for the other. This creates a minor problem for the independent businessman, since usually he finds that data for direct comparison are unavailable from other firm's in his industry. Small, privately held businesses seldom release financial information to competitors. Fortunately, a businessman can obtain comparative standards indirectly and from a number of sources.

The *Annual Statement Studies* prepared by Robert Morris Associates (RMA) provides perhaps the most useful general collection of comparative data for the independent businessman. This national association compiles financial statement data provided by its member bank-loan and credit officers.

Because RMA uses annual sales volume to categorize the most recent comparative data, a business can obtain useful comparative financial criteria for its own circumstances. A small business need not employ comparative standards that are more suitable for larger businesses.

RMA provides a composite *common-size* balance sheet and income statement for each category of businesses. A common-size income statement expresses each account as a percentage of total sales. A common-size balance sheet expresses each account as a percentage of total assets or total liabilities and stockholders' equity. These statements enable a business to compare its own common-size statements to those from its competitors. Figure 5–1 is a representative view showing these comparative criteria for paint, varnish, and lacquer manufacturers.

A third feature in Figure 5–1, RMA's presentation of the ratios, provides the foundation for comparative financial analysis. Note that RMA provides three values for each ratio—the *median,* the *upper quartile,* and the *lower quartile.* The median is the figure that falls in the middle when RMA ranks the ratios for all the firm's within a specific size category. The upper quartile represents the figure halfway between the median and the highest values. The figure halfway between the median and the lowest ratio becomes the lower quartile. By providing three values for each ratio, RMA enables a businessman to compare his firm with the "average" firm, as well as with the typical business in the top and bottom halves of each category.

The median ratio, or statistical average, is a convenient standard for comparative financial analysis. For example, assume a paint manufacturer with a $1 million average sales volume has a two-to-one debt/equity ratio. The RMA median ratio stands at 1:5, which exceeds the comparative standard. Its debt load exceeds the statistical average.

A business may justify a higher debt/equity ratio, but a significant deviation from the norm deserves explanation. Failure to find that explanation should encourage a business to reduce its debt. Otherwise, the firm will operate at a comparative financial disadvantage.

From another perspective, RMA's upper and lower quartile ratios set reasonable financial limits for a business. For example, reviewing the same $250m–$1mm sales category in Figure 5–1, note the 3:1 debt/equity ratio registered by the lower-quartile business. The firm's relative debt burden is higher than that carried by almost 75% of the other businesses in the same category. Perhaps a business can justify a debt/equity ratio that exceeds the industry norm, but exceeding the limit set by the lower-quartile firm inevitably risks financial instability.

On the other hand, the upper-quartile firm's .7 debt/equity ratio marks a practical lower limit on the debt that should be employed by a paint manufacturer. That a lower debt limit exists may come as a surprise to many conservative businessmen. However, the business that uses little or no debt usually generates a below-average return on its stockholders' equity.

Internal Comparative Criteria

Internal comparative analysis focuses on changes apparent in a firm's financial circumstances across successive operating periods. The analysis isolates any unfavorable trends that might call for management action. Internal comparative analysis commonly takes two forms.

One form employs the same financial data a business develops for external comparative analysis. But internal comparative analysis places the ratios in a sequence that matches the order of the firm's operating periods. That helps the perceptive analyst identify developing trends that deserve management attention.

For example, assume that the comparative debt/equity ratio for a business over four successive operating periods is:

Operating Period	1	2	3	4
D/E Ratio	1:6	1:8	2:0	2:2

MANUFACTURERS - PAINT, VARNISH & LACQUER
SIC# 2851

	Current Data 35(6/30-9/30/80) / 120(10/1/80-3/31/81)					ASSET SIZE	Comparative Historical Data				
	0-1MM 34	1-10MM 91	10-50MM 23	50-100MM 7	ALL 155	NUMBER OF STATEMENTS	6/30/76-3/31/77 ALL 154	6/30/77-3/31/78 ALL 147	6/30/78-3/31/79 ALL 129	6/30/79-3/31/80 ALL 148	6/30/80-3/31/81 ALL 155
	%	%	%	%	%	**ASSETS**	%	%	%	%	%
	7.6	7.5	8.3		7.6	Cash & Equivalents	7.9	7.5	6.9	6.5	7.6
	30.9	29.1	29.9		29.6	Accts. & Notes Rec. - Trade(net)	27.6	28.3	34.0	29.4	29.6
	28.6	34.4	25.4		31.4	Inventory	33.3	33.7	34.0	33.1	31.4
	1.7	1.4	1.2		1.4	All Other Current	1.7	1.4	1.5	1.2	1.4
	68.7	72.3	64.9		70.0	Total Current	70.5	70.9	72.4	70.2	70.0
	21.7	20.4	27.6		22.1	Fixed Assets (net)	21.7	21.4	20.7	21.9	22.1
	.8	.5	.8		.6	Intangibles (net)	.8	.7	.7	.9	.6
	8.8	6.8	6.7		7.2	All Other Non-Current	7.0	7.1	6.3	7.1	7.2
	100.0	100.0	100.0		100.0	Total	100.0	100.0	100.0	100.0	100.0
						LIABILITIES					
	7.3	6.9	4.4		6.3	Notes Payable-Short Term	7.8	7.2	7.2	6.6	6.3
	2.4	1.9	1.6		2.0	Cur. Mat.-L/T/D	2.2	2.5	2.7	2.2	2.0
	18.4	17.3	16.2		17.3	Accts. & Notes Payable - Trade	16.1	17.0	19.1	19.3	17.3
	6.8	7.2	7.6		7.2	Accrued Expenses	6.3	7.1	6.9	6.5	7.2
	3.9	2.5	1.9		2.7	All Other Current	3.8	3.0	2.6	3.6	2.7
	38.7	35.9	31.8		35.5	Total Current	36.2	36.8	38.5	38.3	35.5
	13.5	12.2	11.1		12.5	Long Term Debt	12.3	10.9	11.3	12.8	12.5
	1.7	1.7	2.7		2.5	All Other Non-Current	2.0	1.8	1.5	2.3	2.5
	46.0	49.1	54.4		49.5	Net Worth	49.5	50.5	48.7	46.6	49.5
	100.0	100.0	100.0		100.0	Total Liabilities & Net Worth	100.0	100.0	100.0	100.0	100.0
						INCOME DATA					
	100.0	100.0	100.0		100.0	Net Sales	100.0	100.0	100.0	100.0	100.0
	72.4	70.4	67.7		70.4	Cost Of Sales	69.5	69.0	69.8	71.1	70.4
	27.6	29.6	32.3		29.6	Gross Profit	30.5	31.0	30.2	28.9	29.6
	23.9	25.3	25.9		25.0	Operating Expenses	24.5	25.6	25.1	24.3	25.0
	3.7	4.3	6.4		4.6	Operating Profit	6.0	5.4	5.1	4.6	4.6
	.6	.7	.6		.7	All Other Expenses (net)	1.5	.9	1.1	.8	.7
	3.1	3.6	5.8		4.0	Profit Before Taxes	4.5	4.5	4.0	3.8	4.0
						RATIOS					
	2.6	2.7	2.8		2.7	Current	3.1	3.1	2.8	2.5	2.7
	1.9	2.1	2.1		2.1		2.2	2.2	2.0	2.0	2.1
	1.3	1.6	1.8		1.6		1.6	1.6	1.5	1.4	1.6
	1.8	1.6	1.6		1.6	Quick	1.6	1.5	1.4	1.3	1.6
	1.0	1.1	1.1		1.1		1.1	1.1	1.1	1.0	1.1
	.6	.7	.9		.8		.8	.7	.7	.7	.8
	35 10.5	33 10.9	42 8.7		35 10.3	Sales/Receivables	33 11.2	35 11.2	35 10.4	35 10.5	35 10.3
	42 8.6	42 8.6	44 8.3		43 8.4		42 8.6	42 8.2	42 8.1	43 8.6	43 8.4
	51 7.1	54 6.7	55 6.6		54 6.7		56 6.5	57 6.8	55 6.4	54 6.6	54 6.7

Fig. 5-1.

Figures in each ratio cell are shown as upper quartile / median / lower quartile. Values in ( ) are the number of statements used for that ratio. M = $thousand   MM = $million

	34/60/104	49/70/104	55/65/69	48/66/96	58/79/99	57/104	54/74/107	51/69/96	48/66/96
Cost of Sales/Inventory	10.6 / 6.1 / 3.5	7.5 / 5.2 / 3.5	6.6 / 6.6 / 5.3	7.6 / 5.5 / 3.8	6.3 / 4.6 / 3.7	6.4 / 4.6 / 3.5	6.7 / 4.9 / 3.4	7.2 / 5.3 / 3.8	7.6 / 5.5 / 3.8
Sales/Working Capital	5.7 / 7.6 / 12.6	4.6 / 6.5 / 10.9	5.2 / 7.4 / 8.2	4.8 / 7.0 / 10.6	4.5 / 6.4 / 9.8	4.3 / 6.4 / 10.3	4.4 / 7.1 / 11.0	4.7 / 7.6 / 12.1	4.8 / 7.0 / 10.6
EBIT/Interest	13.1 / 5.4 / 2.1 (30)	7.8 / 4.1 / 1.7 (74)	25.1 / 3.8 / 1.5 (20)	9.4 / 4.1 / 1.8 (131)	9.8 / 4.9 / 2.4 (110)	17.6 / 5.5 / 2.8 (95)	11.5 / 5.4 / 1.9 (112)	8.6 / 4.5 / 1.5 (131)	9.4 / 4.1 / 1.8 (131)
Cash Flow/Cur. Mat. L/T/D	6.1 / 3.0 / .9 (18)	9.1 / 4.2 / 1.8 (58)	21.2 / 5.3 / 2.5 (17)	9.8 / 3.9 / 1.9 (100)	7.0 / 3.4 / 1.6 (89)	8.8 / 3.9 / 1.4 (85)	9.5 / 3.5 / 1.6 (90)	9.1 / 3.7 / 1.7 (100)	9.8 / 3.9 / 1.9 (100)
Fixed/Worth	.3 / .4 / .8	.2 / .4 / .6	.3 / .5 / .7	.3 / .4 / .7	.3 / .4 / .7	.2 / .4 / .6	.2 / .4 / .6	.3 / .5 / .7	.3 / .4 / .7
Debt/Worth	.5 / 1.1 / 2.1	.6 / .9 / 2.2	.4 / 1.1 / 1.3	.6 / 1.0 / 1.9	.5 / 1.0 / 1.8	.5 / .9 / 1.6	.6 / 1.1 / 1.8	.6 / 1.1 / 2.0	.6 / 1.0 / 1.9
% Profit Before Taxes/Tangible Net Worth	32.4 / 15.4 / 3.2 (33)	27.9 / 14.8 / 6.8	30.1 / 20.2 / 8.3	30.2 / 16.2 / 6.8 (154)	28.3 / 18.2 / 7.9 (146)	28.6 / 18.4 / 7.4 (128)	30.8 / 16.2 / 8.2 (145)	31.3 / 19.2 / 5.8 (154)	30.2 / 16.2 / 6.8 (154)
% Profit Before Taxes/Total Assets	15.7 / 9.1 / 1.4	15.4 / 7.3 / 2.3	22.5 / 10.1 / 4.1	15.8 / 8.6 / 2.5	14.4 / 8.4 / 3.3	14.7 / 8.2 / 3.1	13.4 / 8.6 / 2.7	15.4 / 8.7 / 2.7	15.8 / 8.6 / 2.5
Sales/Net Fixed Assets	30.7 / 11.9 / 6.8	21.3 / 11.6 / 7.6	11.3 / 7.8 / 6.2	20.3 / 10.3 / 7.1	20.7 / 10.9 / 7.1	22.0 / 11.8 / 7.2	22.2 / 12.1 / 8.0	19.6 / 11.2 / 7.8	20.3 / 10.3 / 7.1
Sales/Total Assets	3.0 / 2.4 / 2.0	2.8 / 2.4 / 1.9	2.4 / 2.2 / 2.0	2.7 / 2.3 / 1.9	2.7 / 2.3 / 1.9	2.7 / 2.3 / 2.0	2.8 / 2.3 / 1.9	2.8 / 2.3 / 1.9	2.7 / 2.3 / 1.9
% Depr., Depr., Amort./Sales	.8 / 1.3 / 1.8 (29)	.8 / 1.2 / 1.7 (83)	1.1 / 1.6 / 1.8 (22)	.8 / 1.3 / 1.8 (141)	.9 / 1.2 / 1.8 (134)	.8 / 1.2 / 1.8 (119)	.8 / 1.2 / 1.7 (131)	.9 / 1.3 / 1.6 (141)	.8 / 1.3 / 1.8 (141)
% Lease & Rental Exp/Sales	1.1 / 1.5 / 2.3 (15)	.5 / 1.0 / 2.5 (40)	.7 / 1.9 / 2.7 (12)	.6 / 1.2 / 2.4 (70)	.6 / 1.2 / 1.8 (62)	.6 / 1.3 / 2.1 (64)	.6 / 1.2 / 1.8 (55)	.6 / 1.1 / 1.9 (70)	.6 / 1.2 / 2.4 (70)
% Officers' Comp/Sales	2.1 / 4.5 / 6.3 (11)	1.1 / 2.4 / 3.7 (30)	1.1 / 2.4 / 3.7	1.2 / 2.7 / 4.5 (43)	1.8 / 2.7 / 4.7 (52)	1.8 / 3.3 / 5.6 (45)	1.9 / 3.4 / 5.2 (44)	1.5 / 3.2 / 4.9 (43)	1.2 / 2.7 / 4.5 (43)
Net Sales ($)	49334M	830101M	1427206M	862405M	1747704M	1790022M	1290338M	1793129M	3169046M
Total Assets ($)	19315M	313664M	641394M	437223M	825533M	868475M	617025M	807121M	1411596M

M = $thousand   MM = $million

Interpretation of Statement Studies Figures

RMA recommends that Statement Studies data be regarded only as general guidelines and not as absolute industry norms. There are several reasons why the data may not be fully representative of a given industry:

(1) The financial statements used in the *Statement Studies* are not selected by any random or statistically reliable method. RMA member banks voluntarily submit the raw data they have available each year, with these being the only constraints: (a) The fiscal year-ends of the companies reported may not be from April 1 through June 29, and (b) their total assets must be less than $100 million.

(2) Many companies have varied product lines; however, the *Statement Studies* categorize them by their primary product Standard Industrial Classification (SIC) number only.

(3) Some of our industry samples are rather small in relation to the total number of firms in a given industry. A relatively small sample can increase the chances that some of our composites do not fully represent an industry.

(4) There is the chance that an extreme statement can be present in a sample, causing a disproportionate influence on the industry composite. This is particularly true in a relatively small sample.

(5) Companies within the same industry may differ in their method of operations which in turn can directly influence their financial statements. Since they are included in our sample, too, these statements can significantly affect our composite calculations.

(6) Other considerations that can result in variations among different companies engaged in the same general line of business are different labor markets; geographical location; different accounting methods; quality of products handled; sources and methods of financing; and terms of sale.

For these reasons, RMA does not recommend the Statement Studies *figures be considered as absolute norms for a given industry. Rather the figures should be used only as general guidelines and in addition to the other methods of financial analysis.*

Fig. 5-2.

Although an increase in the debt/equity ratio weakens a firm's financial condition, external comparative analysis may prove that even the 2:2 ratio falls well within industry standards. Nevertheless, the increase should induce management to control or reverse it.

The other form of internal comparative analysis employs common-size financial statements. Ratio analysis usually provides an adequate view of a firm's financial position, but comparing common-size income statements provides a more detailed perspective.

Common-size statements merely restate the accounts that make up a firm's income statements as a percentage of total sales. Comparative analysis then attempts to isolate trends, either favorable or unfavorable, suggested by changes in any expense category relative to sales.

Note the comparative common-size income statements for Window Manufacturing Company in Table 5–1. The declining net profit as a per-

Table 5-1. Window Manufacturing Company,
Comparative Common-Size Income Statements

	1980	1981	1982
Sales	100.0%	100.0%	100.0%
Cost of Goods Sold	62.0	62.9	64.0
Materials	31.4	32.1	32.9
Labor	15.0	15.9	18.0
Overhead	15.6	14.9	13.2
Gross Profit	38.0	37.1	36.0
Operating Expenses	30.4	32.1	29.8
Selling	10.0	11.2	9.0
General	15.1	15.1	15.1
Administrative	5.3	5.9	5.7
Operating Profit	7.6	5.0	4.8
Interest	.5	1.0	1.1
Profit Before Taxes	7.1	4.0	3.7
Taxes	2.3	1.3	1.2
Net Profit	4.8	2.8	2.5

centage of sales certainly represents an unfavorable trend. At the same time, we can see that the decline stems primarily from the firm's rising cost of goods sold. That cost has risen from 62% of Window Manufacturing's sales in 1980 to 64% in 1982.

Note that the comparison in Table 5–1 includes the underlying accounts that make up Window Manufacturing's cost of goods sold. This allows a better view of the expense categories that deserve management attention. In this instance, rising material and labor costs relative to sales are the financial culprits.

More detailed common-size income statements often include every significant expense category in order to help identify financial trends that may be obscured in summary accounting totals. For example, assume that a firm's material costs relative to sales increase by 5%, while its overhead costs decline by the same relative amount. The firm's relative cost-of-goods-sold total remains the same. The businessman who fails to look beyond the latter relationship allows a favorable financial trend to mask an unfavorable one. Over all, the business is no worse off than before, but the potential for improvement exists.

Common-size income statements fill a natural void left by traditional financial analysis and make a valuable contribution to positive financial management. Of course, the focus of any aspect of financial analysis centers on comparative analysis:

FINANCIAL FACT

Comparative criteria provide the foundation for financial analysis.

In the absence of the appropriate comparative data, many financial ratios and formulas lose much of their potential management value. Before discussing those formulas and ratios, let's review the *Formula Kit*'s unique conceptual approach to financial analysis.

PERSPECTIVES FOR MANAGEMENT

Since financial ratios and formulas are essential management tools, the *Formula Kit*'s approach to financial analysis is designed to contribute directly to positive financial management. That approach focuses on:

1. Performance analysis
2. Component analysis
3. Structural analysis

Performance Analysis

Performance analysis begins with a look at the operating results in a business—the bottom line of the income statement. But any analysis that stops at the bottom line does not provide an adequate assessment of a firm's performance. To emphasize that, we separate performance analysis into two phases.

The first phase applies the basic analytic yardsticks to the income statement to analyze a firm's profit performance. That analysis does concentrate on the bottom line, but other measures of profit performance are also important.

A firm's net profits cannot be evaluated properly without also looking at its operating profits. A large interest burden can make net profits unsatisfactory, while operating profits may meet industry standards. Nor can conclusions be drawn from looking at operating profits without also examining gross profits. Below-average operating expenses can conceal a gross profit margin that falls below industry standards. Indeed, analyzing profit performance requires evaluation of every level of a firm's operating results.

The second phase of performance analysis evaluates management. A satisfactory profit performance does not necessarily represent a satisfactory management performance. A business that apparently is doing well might do better. An evaluation of management's performance relies primarily on two key financial ratios. One ratio measures the return a business earns on its stockholders' equity. The other gauges how efficiently management employs the assets. Both help distinguish management performance from profit performance.

Evaluation devices often orient the management objectives in a business, but the profit-performance gauge ultimately provides the focal point for positive financial management. Managing assets more efficiently naturally increases earnings and pushes up the return on the stockholders' equity.

Component Analysis

Component analysis views each of a firm's major asset accounts as a separate profit center. Thus better inventory management can improve earnings, even though sales remain constant. The same benefit accrues from more efficient accounts receivable and fixed-asset management. In fact, the premise that justifies component analysis suggests that increasing sales is not the only way to improve a firm's operating performance.

Practical limits exist on how efficiently a business can manage its assets. Reducing inventory too much can seriously damage sales. Excessive credit restrictions can drive perspective customers to competitors. Certainly, financial trade-offs exist. Nevertheless, the information derived from component analysis makes a valuable contribution to positive financial management.

Structural Analysis

Structural analysis examines the more important interrelationships among the financial elements that make up a firm's balance sheet, as well as the interrelationship among those elements and the income statement. After all, the most efficient asset management does not preclude financial problems for the business with an unbalanced financial structure.

Structural analysis concentrates on two specific characteristics of a firm's financial position: liquidity and leverage. Liquidity measures cash capability and estimates a firm's ability to meet its obligations promptly. It also indicates how financial traumas can develop from illiquidity. Sensible liquidity management becomes a logical complement to sensible component management.

Leverage analysis focuses on the debt employed by a business. Excessive debt creates an unbalanced financial structure and raises the potential for serious financial problems.

Indeed, no aspect of financial analysis stands alone. No analytic perspective provides all of the answers necessary to orient sensible financial management decisions. Positive financial management requires the whole analytic package.

SECTION TWO
Performance Analysis

6 Analyzing Profit Performance

Evaluating profit performance is a logical starting point for financial analysis. Few conclusions can be drawn directly from dollar profit figures, however. Knowing that a firm's net income after taxes totals $100,000 doesn't tell us whether that performance is good or bad. The figure becomes important only when we measure those results as a percentage of the firm's total sales. A complete evaluation requires a look at all four perspectives of the profits generated by a business:

1. Gross profit margin
2. Operating profit margin
3. Pretax profit margin
4. Net profit margin

Table 6–1 presents the comparative income statements that summarize the financial progress by the Galvez Manufacturing Company during the years ending 12/31/81 and 12/31/82. Galvez manufactures paint products, so we can also incorporate the RMA comparative data from Table 5–1 into the discussion.

Table 6-1. Galvez Manufacturing Company

	1981	1982
	(1981 and 1982 income statements)	
Sales	$1,035,000	$1,185,000
Cost of Goods Sold	641,700	750,500
Gross Profit	$ 393,300	$ 434,500
Operating Expenses	325,300	361,200
Operating Income (EBIT)	$ 68,000	$ 73,300
Interest Expenses	10,200	13,100
Earnings Before Taxes (EBT)	$ 57,800	$ 60,200
Taxes*	11,590	12,310
Net Income	$ 46,210	$ 47,890

*17% of first $25,000 in taxable income; 20% of next $25,000; and 30% over $50,000.

THE GROSS PROFIT MARGIN

The difference between the total sales during an operating period and the cost of the goods sold measures a firm's gross profits. Relating that difference to the sales total provides the first measure of profit performance:

$$\text{Gross Profit Margin} = \frac{\text{Sales} - \text{Cost of Goods Sold}}{\text{Sales}}$$

Note that the gross profits can be substituted directly from the income statement for the numerator in the calculation. However, the approach here isolates the two major factors that interrelate to produce the gross profits in a business.

The equation for the Galvez Company's 1982 income statement would be:

$$\text{Gross Profit Margin} = \frac{\$1,185,000 - \$750,500}{\$1,185,000}$$

$$\text{Gross Profit Margin} = \frac{\$ 434,500}{\$1,185,000} = \mathbf{36.7}$$

The average Galvez Company sales dollar contributed almost thirty-seven cents to the firm's total gross profits in 1982. But what management implications arise from the financial interrelationships that produced that margin?

Analyzing the Gross Profit Margin

The gross profit margin in a business develops from the interrelationship between a firm's price structure and its purchase and production costs. An inadequate gross profit margin implies that a firm's product costs are too high or its prices too low. In this instance, the data in Table 5–1 show that the Galvez Company's gross profit margin compares favorably with the 29.6% industry standard for similar firms.

The evaluation of the gross profit margin also should include a look at any variation in that margin across successive operating periods. Using the same calculation process, we find that the Galvez Company generated a 38% gross profit margin in 1981. So the 1982 margin actually represents a 1.3% drop from the previous year. Despite the company's comparative edge over the industry standard, that decrease deserves explanation. That explanation can be found by comparing the percentage increase in sales in 1982 with the percentage rise in the firm's cost of goods sold (CGS). The comparative percentage develops from the calculations:

$$\frac{\% \text{ Increase}}{\text{in Sales}} = \frac{1982 \text{ Sales} - 1981 \text{ Sales}}{1981 \text{ Sales}} = \frac{\$1,185,000 - \$1,035,000}{\$1,035,000} = \textbf{14.5\%}$$

$$\frac{\% \text{ Increase}}{\text{in CGS}} = \frac{1982 \text{ CGS} - 1981 \text{ CGS}}{1981 \text{ CGS}} = \frac{\$750,500 - \$641,700}{\$641,700} = \textbf{17.0\%}$$

The Galvez Company's product costs rose 2.5% more rapidly than the firm's prices in 1982. That naturally results in a smaller gross profit margin.

Of course, we lack the information necessary to identify the actual financial culprit here. The problem might stem from inadequate cost controls, or the company might need to pass inflationary increases in product costs onto its customers by pushing up its sales prices. But the analysis provides a view of a potential problem that deserves management attention.

THE OPERATING PROFIT MARGIN

A firm's operating expenses include all of the costs incurred from normal operations, apart from those associated with the cost of goods sold.* Deducting those expenses from gross profits measures the firm's operating profits. Relating those profits to total sales enables us to evaluate the performance measured by the gains from the firm's overall operations. The calculation becomes:

$$\text{Operating Profit Margin} = \frac{\text{Operating Profits (EBIT)}}{\text{Sales}}$$

The Galvez Company's operating profit for 1982 is:

$$\text{Operating Profit Margin} = \frac{\$\ \ 73,300}{\$1,185,000} = \textbf{6.2\%}$$

The company's operations produced 6.2¢ in profits from each sales dollar in 1982. Let's see how that serves as a gauge of the firm's operating effectiveness.

Analyzing the Operating Profit Margin

Operating expenses do not include the cost of any borrowed funds or income taxes. Consequently, the operating profit margin is the best measure of a firm's ability to make any financial gains.

Another glance at Table 5–1 indicates that the Galvez Company's 6.2% operating profit margin falls below the 7.0% average among comparable firms in its industry. The company's competitors apparently operate more efficiently. However, a better view of a firm's operating results can be obtained by interrelating the operating profit margin with the gross profit margin. After all, a firm's operating profits follow deductions for both the cost of goods sold and operating costs. Effective cost control in one area can disguise ineffective cost control in another, even though the operating profit margin appears satisfactory.

The Galvez Company's 36.7% gross profit margin in 1982 stood well above the 30.8% average for comparable firms. Consequently, the firm's

---

*Remember that interest charges and income taxes do not fall into the operating-expense category.

below-average operating profit margin represents a more severe discrepancy than the .8% differential first suggests. Excessive selling, distribution, and administrative costs offset the benefits from the firm's more efficient manufacturing operations.

The Galvez Company's management should be concerned about the substandard operating profit margin, since the 6.2% operating profit margin in 1982 represents a .3% decline from the previous year. The drop can be attributed to the decline in the gross profit margin, but that merely emphasizes that management cannot rely on efficient product cost control alone to preserve its operating profit margin. Effective operating-cost control also is important.

The operating profit margin provides the best measure of a firm's overall profit performance. But a firm's financing decisions, how management chooses to fund operations, has a significant impact on the final earnings total the business finally realizes. The pretax profit margin registers that impact.

THE PRETAX PROFIT MARGIN

Borrowed funds enter into the financial structure of almost every business enterprise, but the interest charges for those funds stand apart from a firm's product costs and operating expenses. To identify earnings before taxes (EBT), those charges are deducted from the operating profits. Then those earnings are related to total sales to find the pretax profit margin:

$$\text{Pretax Profit Margin} = \frac{\text{Earnings Before Taxes}}{\text{Sales}}$$

In the Galvez Company's circumstance, the pretax profit margin in 1982 becomes:

$$\text{Pretax Profit Margin} = \frac{\$\ 60,200}{\$1,185,000} = \textbf{5.1\%}$$

The Galvez Company's financing charges lowered the firm's pretax profit margin to 5.1% of its sales. Since a business seldom has significant influence on the income taxes extracted from its earnings, the pretax profit margin provides perhaps the best measure of a firm's actual earnings.

Analyzing the Pretax Profit Margin

A firm's financial structure has a significant influence on its profit performance. The more debt a business employs, the larger that influence becomes. However, just because interest charges reduce the pretax earnings total on an income statement does not mean that a business should avoid using borrowed funds. Indeed, a business easily can justify borrowing, and the interest charges that proceed from the proper use of debt can be beneficial.

The increase in operating profits that develops from borrowed funds easily can exceed the accompanying interest charges. Borrowed funds also can increase the proportionate return a business provides to its stockholders. That holds true even though using equity in place of debt might increase the firm's earnings total.

Table 5–1 shows that the Galvez Company's 5.1% pretax profit margin stands slightly above the 4.9% industry standard. We previously noted that the Galvez Company operating profit margin fell below the industry standard. So the firm's interest charges apparently aren't damaging its profit performance, presuming that the borrowed funds are used to contribute to earnings.

We should recognize the signal that indicates excessive interest charges. It appears when those charges translate a satisfactory operating profit margin into an unsatisfactory pretax profit margin. Further analysis may justify that circumstance over a short-term period, but it should remind you of the need to examine all of the factors that enter into profit performance.

THE NET PROFIT MARGIN

Net profits represent the final measure of a firm's financial performance after recognizing its income-tax obligation. The net profit margin evaluates the firm's overall ability to squeeze profits from each sales dollar. The net profit margin can be identified in a similar way to the other profit margin calculations:

$$\text{Net Profit Margin} = \frac{\text{Net Profits}}{\text{Sales}}$$

The Galvez Company's net profit margin in 1982 appears as:

$$\text{Net Profit Margin} = \frac{\$\ \ 47,890}{\$1,185,000} = \textbf{4.0\%}$$

Four cents out of each Galvez Company sales dollar finally reached the firm's bottom line.

Analyzing the Net Profit Performance

Expanding the net profit margin is a primary business objective, even though standing alone it provides little useful information for management. Solving any mystery about a firm's net profit performance requires a look at the factors that determine the other three profit margins. In fact, the RMA industry data in Table 5–1 does not include comparative net profit margin figures because the tax system often affects different businesses unevenly. So net profit margins are less reliable standards for comparison. The omission reminds us that any management analysis of a firm's profit performance must proceed beyond the obvious measure of its net profit margin. That warrants recognition in:

FINANCIAL FACT

8

Analyzing a firm's profit
performance requires a look
at all four views
of its profit margins.

7 Analyzing Management Performance

A satisfactory profit performance does not prove that a business enjoys effective management. A business with inept management may generate good profit margins simply because it has the right product in the right market at the right time. Evaluating management performance requires a look *beyond* a firm's profit margins and toward two interrelated performance gauges.

One gauge relates a firm's net profits to the accounting value of its stockholders' equity and measures the proportionate return those profits provide to each equity dollar. Naturally, a better management performance produces a higher return on the stockholders' equity, or return on equity (ROE). However, even a poorly managed business that suffers from a below-average profit performance can generate an above-average ROE. This is because borrowed funds can magnify the returns a firm's profits represent to its stockholders. That effect also can benefit the stockholders in a well-managed business. But the potential for a distorting influence from borrowed funds makes the ROE calculation a less reliable gauge of management performance.

The second gauge, the return on investment (ROI) calculation, reduces that distorting influence because it relates a firm's earnings to the total assets employed to generate those earnings. Usually, a higher ROI represents a better management performance.

Moreover, a direct relationship exists between the ROI in a business and the return on its equity. A higher ROI translates directly into a higher ROE. Consequently, ROI should become a focal point of positive financial management.

RETURN ON INVESTMENT (ROI)
AND RETURN ON EQUITY (ROE)

Table 7–1 presents the comparative balance sheets for the Galvez Manufacturing Company at 12/31/81 and 12/31/82. Subsequent analysis of those financial statements will raise numerous questions about the firm's financial circumstances. However, only two aspects of the statements are relevant

Table 7-1. Galvez Manufacturing Company,
Comparative Balance Sheets

	12/31/81	12/31/82
Cash	$ 25,000	$ 10,000
Accounts Receivable	205,000	265,000
Inventory	352,500	335,000
Fixed Assets (net of depreciation)	50,000	105,000
Other Assets	15,000	20,000
Total Assets	$647,500	$735,000
Accounts Payable	$272,400	$241,000
Notes Payable (current)	75,000	150,000
Accrued Liabilities	13,500	19,510
Total Current Liabilities	$360,900	$410,510
Notes Payable (long-term)	40,000	30,000
Total Liabilities	$400,900	$440,510
Common Stock	100,000	100,000
Retained Earnings	146,600	194,490
Total Liabilities and Net Worth	$647,500	$735,000

here: What elements enter into the calculation process that identifies return on equity (ROE) and return on investment (ROI)?

The Galvez Company's assets totaled $647,500 and $735,000 on 12/31/81 and 12/31/82, respectively. The stockholders' equity amounted to $246,600 on 12/31/81 and $294,490 on 12/31/82. Those totals represent the accounting measure of the stockholders' interest in the firm's assets. Let's see how these items enter into the evaluation of management performance.

CALCULATING ROE

The income statement measures the profits a business generates for its stockholders. However, stockholders should view those profits from the investor's perspective and focus on the return those profits represent relative to the equity funds committed to the enterprise. That perspective develops from the calculation:

$$ROE = \frac{\text{Net Profits}}{\text{Stockholders' Equity}}$$

The stockholders' equity in the Galvez Company totaled $246,600 on 12/31/81. This includes the stockholders' initial investment, as well as all of the previous earnings retained in the business. The return on that equity provided by the company's $47,890 in net profits in 1982 is:

$$ROE = \frac{\$\ 47,890}{\$246,600} = \textbf{19.4\%}$$

The company's earnings in 1982 represent a 19.4¢ return for each equity dollar invested on 12/31/81. In the absence of any dividend payments, that translates into a 19.4% increase in the accounting value of the stockholders' equity.

Before examining ROE as a gauge of management performance, we first should eliminate a potential source of confusion associated with the ROE calculation process: that is, the denominator in the calculation employs the stockholders' equity total as it stands at the *beginning* of the business year. While that may appear obvious, some analysts use the year-end equity total as the denominator, including a firm's earnings for the year. Others use an average equity total, since earnings accrue incrementally throughout the year. However, both methods distort a straightforward perspective of the return a firm's earnings represent for its stockholders. Using the equity total as it stands at the beginning of the business year provides a more consistent criterion for evaluating management's performance.

Analyzing ROE

The stockholders in any business expect a yield from their investment. The ROE calculation measures the yield a firm's earnings represent relative to the accounting value of the investment. From an investor's perspective, that return is more important than a firm's net profit margin. Moreover, ROE also becomes an important standard for evaluating management's performance.

Analyzing ROE is seldom a straightforward task. The analysis should begin with a look at comparative industry standards (not included in the RMA data in Table 5–1), but in this instance, those standards may not provide reliable comparative criteria. A comparatively low ROE does not prove that a business suffers from inept management. Nor is a high ROE irrefutable evidence that a business enjoys effective management. In any circumstance, the evaluation process must recognize the interrelationship between a firm's financial structure and the return it generates on the stockholders' equity.

To demonstrate that interrelationship, let's compare two businesses that generate $200,000 in operating profits (EBIT). Both businesses employ $600,000 in total assets, but they have different financial structures. One business employs no debt, while the other uses $300,000 in borrowed funds. The comparative financial structures appear as:

	Firm 1	Firm 2
Total Assets	$600,000	$600,000
Total Liabilities	—	300,000
Stockholders' Equity	600,000	300,000
Liabilities and Equity	$600,000	$600,000

Firm 2 pays a 12% annual interest charge for its borrowed funds. Consequently, we can complete the comparative earnings and ROE totals for the two firms:

	Firm 1	Firm 2
Operating Profits (EBIT)	$200,000	$200,000
Interest Expenses	—	(36,000)
Profits Before Taxes	$200,000	$164,000
Taxes (30% average rate)	(60,000)	(49,200)
Net Profits	$140,000	$114,800
Return on equity (ROE)	23.3%	38.3%

The absence of debt allows Firm 1 to register higher net profits. Yet the stockholders in Firm 2 enjoy a significantly higher return on their equity. That provides an important view of the positive contribution debt can make to a business, but it also demonstrates that the return a business generates on its stockholders' equity cannot stand alone as a gauge of management performance. Indeed, management can use debt to magnify a modest profit performance into a ROE total that stands well above any comparative standard.

Generating a higher return on the stockholders' equity is always a desirable objective, and within realistic limits, using debt to achieve that objective represents a reasonable management practice. But that practice also can create a distorted measure of management's performance. Nevertheless, the ROE calculation is a valuable device for evaluating management:

FINANCIAL FACT

9

The ROE calculation
measures the yield
that a firm's earnings represent
for its stockholders.

A satisfactory profit performance that leaves stockholders with a low return on their equity should raise a question about management's overall performance. In the absence of any other standard, stockholders should compare a firm's ROE to the yield available from alternative investment opportunities. That comparison may provide a better criterion for gauging management performance than the prevailing industry standard. In any event, the return on investment criterion provides an even better perspective of management performance.

CALCULATING ROI

The net profit margin measures the average return a business earns from each sales dollar. The ROE calculation identifies the yield the firm's cumulative earnings represent for its stockholders. But neither calculation measures how effectively management employs the dollars invested in assets. The ROI calculation gauges that effectiveness:

$$ROI = \frac{Net\ Profits}{Total\ Assets}$$

We can assess how efficiently the Galvez Company's management employed the firm's assets in 1982:

$$ROI = \frac{\$\ 47,890}{\$735,000} = \textbf{6.5\%}$$

The Galvez Company's earnings represent a 6.5% return from each dollar invested in the firm's assets. Remember that the debt employed in the company's financial structure magnified that ROI into a 19.4% return on the stockholders' equity. However, the ROI calculation ignores that debt, except for the reduction in profits that develop from the interest charges. So by relating net profits directly to the total assets available to generate a return, the ROI calculation provides a better measure of management's actual operating effectiveness. In fact, the interrelationships that determine the ROI in a business encompass almost every aspect of its operations.

There is an alternative approach to calculating ROI that ignores the impact interest costs and income taxes have on a firm's profits. That calculation relates a firm's operating profits to its total assets:

$$\frac{Operating\ Return}{on\ Investment} = \frac{Operating\ Profit\ (EBIT)}{Total\ Assets}$$

Remember that interest charges and income taxes do not result directly from a firm's operations, so this calculation provides an undistorted measure of management's operating effectiveness. Of course, management also influences the interest costs and income taxes a business incurs. Consequently, relating net profits to total assets provides a better perspective of management performance and a better criterion for orienting positive financial management.

Analyzing ROI

The assets owned by a business represent an investment, regardless of the mixture of debt and equity that provides the funds invested in those assets. Thus those assets should generate a large enough return to justify continuing the investment. Should the return on that investment fall too low, the funds should be invested elsewhere. The return a business generates from its assets should be a major management concern, since the financial interrelationships that determine the ROI are subject to direct management influence. The ROI calculation provides a summary view of management's impact on those relationships. Another look at the calculation emphasizes that.

The numerator in the ROI calculation actually develops from the net profit margin held in each sales dollar. Holding a firm's total assets constant, any management effort that expands that margin naturally translates into a higher return on that investment. For example, assume that a business presently employs $500,000 in assets to generate a $1 million annual sales volume. A 5% net profit margin produces $50,000 in earnings and a 10% return on investment ($50,000 ÷ $500,000). Any management action that expands the size of that profit margin will increase the firm's earnings. That increase also will produce a higher ROI for the business. Thus a 10% profit margin will push up the firm's earnings to $100,000 and raise its ROI to 20% ($100,000 ÷ $500,000).

Alternatively, the denominator in the ROI calculation reflects management's ability to employ a firm's assets efficiently. As management employs those assets more efficiently, the total investment necessary to conduct any specific sales volume drops. Holding the profit margin in those sales constant, that again creates a higher ROI for the business.

Assume that the Galvez Company's initial 5% profit margin is not subject to expansion. Perhaps competitive pressure precludes any sales price hikes, while inflationary pressure prevents any reduction in expenses.

Nevertheless, more efficient asset management can still increase the firm's ROI.

Now assume that the company's management effort enables the firm to generate the same $1 million sales volume with only a $250,000 total asset investment. The $50,000 in net profits then represents a 20% ROI for the business ($50,000 ÷ $250,000). Thus the size of a firm's ROI is not a function of profits alone. Instead, ROI directly reflects management's ability to generate profits while also employing the firm's assets efficiently. The conscientious businessman cannot ignore either without jeopardizing his firm's ROI.

A critical distinction enters into ROI analysis: Any increase in earnings that develops from a higher sales volume does not automatically translate into a better return from the firm's asset investment. That benefit develops only when the business achieves the sales increase without a concomitant expansion in assets. Indeed, sales volume becomes, at least conceptually, a less significant concern in positive financial management. Instead, as shown in Figure 7–1, that effort focuses on the ROI that develops from the interrelationship between a firm's profit margin and the asset investment employed to generate that margin.

By any standard, the Galvez Company's 6.5% ROI in 1982 represents an inadequate yield from the firm's assets. We noted in Chapter 6 that the

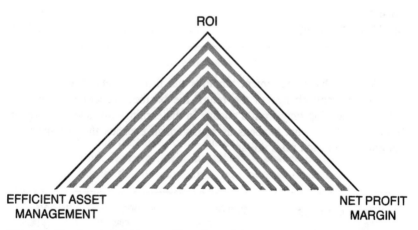

Fig. 7-1. The focal point for positive financial management.

Total Assets	$250,000
Total Liabilities	$125,000
Stockholder's Equity	$125,000
Liabilities and Equity	$250,000

Presuming that more efficient asset management is not possible, let's see what happens as wider profit margins raise the firm's earnings:

Earnings	$25,000	50,000	75,000
ROI	10%	20%	30%
ROE	20%	40%	60%

This confirms that debt does not alter the direct relationship between the ROI and ROE. Also, using debt to finance 50% of a firm's assets doubles the impact any change in the ROI has on the ROE. Using larger proportions of debt magnifies that impact even more; the effect decreases as debt occupies a smaller proportion of a firm's financial structure.

Note that to simplify the discussion we did not attribute any direct cost to the debt, and presumably we can ignore that cost since net earnings after interest and taxes are used in the return calculations. At the same time, the cost of borrowing naturally enters into any decision to use debt in a firm's financial structure. Here we emphasize the benefits stockholders enjoy whenever a business generates a higher return from its assets. The businessman who recognizes those benefits will remember:

FINANCIAL FACT

Return on investment
provides the focal point
for positive
financial management.

ROI is the most important criterion for evaluating management performance. It reflects management's ability to generate profits while using the firm's assets efficiently.

SECTION THREE
Component Analysis

8 Investment in Accounts Receivable

Manufacturers and wholesalers sell merchandise in exchange for their customers' promise to pay later, or accounts receivable, rather than for cash. Consequently, the accumulated receivables outstanding at any time typically represents a significant proportion of the total dollars invested in a firm's assets. This chapter reviews the factors that determine the size of that investment.

FORMULAS FOR ANALYSIS

Regardless of sales volume, a smaller total asset investment can improve the ROI in a business. So ideally a business should sell only for cash, which would eliminate the need for any investment in accounts receivable. Not only do few businesses do that, but requiring cash payment for all purchases eliminates many prospective customers who expect credit consideration. That limits sales, reduces profits, and lowers the return a business can generate from its assets.

The decision to extend credit consideration and carry the resulting investment in accounts receivable focuses on a trade-off. The trade-off compares the cost of carrying the investment in accounts receivable against the benefits that develop from a larger sales volume. The contribution to a firm's

ROI that develops from the incremental sales must exceed the incremental costs associated with a larger investment in accounts receivable.

The same trade-off exists whenever a business considers a change in the factors that determine the investment in accounts receivable, regardless of the level of sales. Any change in those factors will induce a simultaneous, if not proportionate, increase or decrease in the firm's sales and receivables. So anticipating the impact on ROI becomes a necessary precedent to any management decision affecting the size of a firm's investment in accounts receivable.

The incremental earnings that develop from a larger sales volume can justify an investment in accounts receivable. Two calculations measure that investment:

1. Accounts-receivable turnover rate
2. Average collection period

Both calculations relate the size of a firm's investment in accounts receivable to its total sales volume. A smaller investment relative to a particular sales volume produces a better yield from assets.

THE ACCOUNTS-RECEIVABLE TURNOVER RATE

The accounts-receivable turnover rate calculation gauges how often a business recycles each dollar invested in its accounts receivable over the course of the year:

$$\frac{\text{Accounts-Receivable}}{\text{Turnover Rate}} = \frac{\text{Annual Sales}}{\text{Accounts Receivable}}$$

Relating the Galvez Company's $265,000 investment in accounts receivable on 12/31/82 to its $1,185,000 sales volume for that year:

$$\frac{\text{Accounts-Receivable}}{\text{Turnover Rate}} = \frac{\$1,185,000}{\$\ \ 265,000} = \textbf{4.5}$$

The Galvez Company collected and reinvested each dollar included in its receivables 4.5 times during 1982. Table 5–1 notes that the comparative industry average accounts-receivable turnover rate is 8.6 times per year.

Since the Galvez Company's turnover rate is well below that standard, the firm apparently has an excess investment in accounts receivable. This partially explains the poor average yield from the firm's asset investment identified in Chapter 7. Indeed, the potential reduction in accounts receivable from a higher turnover rate can improve the Galvez Company's ROI.

At any sales level, a higher turnover rate shrinks a firm's investment in accounts receivable and improves the average yield from its assets. A simple illustration, showing an abbreviated view of the MBA Company's financial structure, demonstrates those facts:

Accounts Receivable	$300,000
Other Assets	300,000
Total Assets	$600,000
Stockholders' Equity	$600,000

During the upcoming year, management expects to produce $90,000 in earnings from the MBA Company's projected $1,200,000 sales volume. That earnings total will represent a 15% yield from the firm's total asset investment ($90,000 on $600,000). Of course, MBA's management explored the potential for increasing that yield.

Any increase in the MBA Company's projected sales or profits appears doubtful. Consequently, management focused on the potential benefits that could be derived from more efficient asset utilization. Among other possibilities, it projected the increase in MBA's ROI that would develop from more rapid accounts-receivable turnover rates.

Since the MBA Company doesn't employ any debt, the funds released by reducing MBA's receivable investment presumably would flow directly to the stockholders as an equity refund. This assumption is unrealistic, but it will help clarify the direct relationship between the accounts-receivable turnover rate and the return a business generates from its assets. Table 8–1 demonstrates that relationship.

MBA management's analysis recognized that the firm presently turns its accounts receivable four times in the course of a year ($1,200,000 ÷ 4 = $300,000). With $300,000 in other assets, that turnover rate leaves the MBA

Table 8-1. Accounts-Receivable Turnover Rate and ROI;
the MBA Company

Annual Turnover Rate	Investment in Accounts Receivable	Total Assets	(ROI)
4	$300,000	$600,000	15.0%
5	240,000	540,000	16.7%
6	200,000	500,000	18.0%
7	171,428	471,428	19.9%
8	150,000	450,000	20.0%

Company with the 15% return on its total asset investment. The following calculation identifies the impact that higher turnover rates will have on MBA's investment in receivables:

$$\frac{\text{Investment in}}{\text{Accounts Receivable}} = \frac{\text{Projected Sales}}{\text{Projected Turnover Rate}}$$

Increasing MBA's turnover rate from four to five times per year will reduce the firm's investment in accounts receivable to the $240,000 total in Table 8–1:

$$\frac{\text{Investment in}}{\text{Accounts Receivable}} = \frac{\$1,200,000}{5} = \mathbf{\$240,000}$$

Naturally, any drop in accounts receivable reduces the asset total that enters into the denominator of the ROI calculation. That increases the ROI any level of earnings represent for a business.

The final step in the analytic process relates the MBA Company's $90,000 in earnings to the shrinking asset totals in Table 8–1. Management can increase MBA's ROI to 16.7% by increasing the accounts-receivable turnover rate from four to five times per year. Accelerating that rate up to eight times per year will produce a 20% return from the firm's remaining asset base. Recycling the dollars invested in the firm's receivables even more rapidly will push that yield still higher.

Although there are limits on how rapidly a business can turn its investment in accounts receivable, the MBA Company's circumstance demonstrates the potential benefits a business can obtain by employing the dollars invested in its accounts receivable more efficiently.

THE AVERAGE COLLECTION PERIOD

The collection-period calculation measures how long a firm's average sales dollar remains as an accounts receivable. A longer average collection period creates a larger investment in accounts receivable. The average collection period is identified in the calculation:

$$\text{Average Collection Period} = \frac{360}{\text{Accounts-Receivable Turnover Rate}}$$

Using the Galvez Company's annual turnover rate that was calculated previously:

$$\text{Average Collection Period} = \frac{360}{4.5} = \textbf{80 days}$$

The average Galvez Company sales dollar remains outstanding as an account receivable for eighty days. That collection period far exceeds the forty-two-day industry standard in Table 5–1 and supports the suggestion that the firm's low ROI is partially attributable to an excess investment in accounts receivable. A shorter average collection period reduces the investment in receivables that develops from sales.

A useful alternative approach to calculating the average collection period proceeds in two steps:

1. Divide annual sales by 360 to determine the average daily sales volume
2. Divide the accounts receivable total by the average daily sales volume to identify the average collection period

The data from the Galvez Company can be used to illustrate the calculation process.

$$(1) \quad \frac{\text{Average Daily}}{\text{Sales Volume}} = \frac{\$1,185,000}{360} = \mathbf{\$3,292}$$

$$(2) \quad \frac{\text{Average Collection}}{\text{Period}} = \frac{\text{Accounts Receivable}}{\dfrac{\text{Average Daily}}{\text{Sales Volume}}} = \frac{\$265,000}{\$\ 3,292} = \mathbf{80\ days}$$

This agrees with the average collection period identified above.

This average collection-period calculation is particularly useful for a firm whose sales occur seasonally. In this case, the most recent quarter's sales should be used in place of annual volume in the calculation process. For example, assume a business with a $1.2 million annual sales volume presently has a $250,000 investment in receivables. Based on the annual volume, either calculation process will show that the business has a seventy-five-day average collection period. However, in this instance, we find that $700,000 of the $1.2 million annual sales volume occurs in the final three months of the year. So a more realistic measure of the firm's average collection period can be obtained by focusing on that quarter's sales:

$$\frac{\text{Average Daily}}{\text{Sales Volume}} = \frac{\$700,000}{90} = \mathbf{\$7,778}$$

$$\frac{\text{Average Collection}}{\text{Period}} = \frac{\$250,000}{\$\ 7,778} = \mathbf{32\ days}$$

Thus the apparent excess investment in receivables actually reflects the seasonal characteristics of the firm's sales. That provides a more realistic accounts-receivable management perspective.

Conceptually, the turnover-rate and collection-period calculations provide the same information, since a business with an excess investment in accounts receivable will have both a low turnover rate and a lengthy average collection period. As the business increases its accounts-receivable turnover rate, its average collection period naturally shrinks.

The collection-period calculation provides a useful perspective for managing a firm's investment in accounts receivable. A businessman can easily relate that perspective directly to the credit and collection policies that determine the length of the firm's average collection period. In addition, the average collection period provides a better view of the increase or decrease in receivables management should anticipate from any change in those policies.

PERSPECTIVE FOR ACCOUNTS-RECEIVABLE MANAGEMENT

The average daily sales volume a business generates naturally affects the size of its investment in accounts receivable. A larger sales volume creates a larger investment. However, holding any daily sales volume constant, the size of that investment becomes directly attributable to the length of a firm's average collection period. The calculation that defines that relationship:

$$\frac{\text{Average Daily}}{\text{Sales Volume}} \times \frac{\text{Average Collection}}{\text{Period}} = \frac{\text{Investment in}}{\text{Accounts Receivable}}$$

Thus a business with a $2,500 daily sales volume and a fifty-day average collection period will develop a $125,000 investment in accounts receivable:

$$\$2,500 \times 50 = \textbf{\$125,000}$$

This direct relationship clarifies the conceptual link between a firm's credit and collection policies and the size of its investment in accounts receivable. It becomes apparent that a business can reduce its investment in receivables by implementing more stringent policies that shorten its average collection period. For example, assume that more stringent credit and collection policies reduce the firm's average collection period to forty days. Presuming that the $2,500 daily sales volume remains constant, the firm's investment in accounts receivables will drop to $100,000 ($2,500 × 40).

Alternatively, the lengthier average collection period that develops from more liberal credit and collection policies will expand a firm's investment in accounts receivable. Assume that such policies extend the firm's average collection period to sixty days. Presuming that the $2,500 average daily volume remains unchanged, the firm's investment in accounts receivable rises to $150,000 ($2,500 × 60).

As illustrated in the MBA Company's circumstance, the same relationship can be demonstrated by using comparative accounts-receivable turnover rates. However, the management implications that arise from that relationship become more apparent when we focus on the average collection period. Another look at Table 8–1 helps emphasize that fact. A more rapid accounts receivable turnover rate reduces a firm's investment in accounts and increases its ROI. But the potential for actually accelerating MBA's accounts-receivable turnover rate remains unclear. The task may be relatively simple, or it may represent a formidable management challenge.

The potential for reducing the MBA Company's investment in receivables becomes more apparent when comparative average collection periods are included in the analysis. Using the different levels of accounts receivable in Table 8–1:

Investment in Accounts Receivable	Average Collection Period (days)
$300,000	90
240,000	72
200,000	60
171,428	51
150,000	45

Now we see that the MBA Company's present investment in accounts receivable results from a ninety-day average collection period, which far exceeds almost every industry norm. Consequently, any management effort to implement more stringent credit and collection policies should bring about a significant reduction in the firm's investment in accounts receivables.

The turnover rate calculation remains a useful gauge of management efficiency, but the discussion here demonstrates:

FINANCIAL FACT

The average collection period
provides the best perspective
for managing a firm's investment
in accounts receivable.

This will become more apparent in Chapter 9, where alternative approaches for increasing the return on investment in receivables is discussed. But first, let's examine the critical role accounts receivable play as a source of cash.

CONTRIBUTION TO CASH FLOW

Customer payments on account, rather than sales, represent the primary source of cash for a business. So a better cash flow develops whenever a business employs the dollars invested in its accounts receivable more efficiently. And a shorter average collection period means a better cash flow.

Assume that a profitable business presently generates a $3,000 daily sales volume. Unfortunately, a sixty-day average collection period leaves the firm with a tight cash flow. Extracting the cash and accounts receivable accounts from the firm's most recent balance sheet highlights the problem:

Cash	$ 3,000
Accounts Receivable	$180,000

Certainly, a $3,000 cash operating balance is inadequate for any business generating a $90,000 monthly sales volume. The firm has little defense against any unforeseen financial setback.

The accelerated cash flow that develops from a shorter average collection period can cure the problem. For example, assume that a more conscientious collection effort reduces the firm's average collection period from sixty to forty-five days. The cash and receivable accounts then appear as:

Cash	$ 48,000
Accounts Receivable	$135,000

The fifteen-day reduction in the average collection period shrinks the firm's investment in accounts receivable by $45,000 ($3,000 × 15). But the more significant benefit from the shorter average collection period appears as a simultaneous $45,000 increase in the cash account. The business no longer suffers from a cash deficiency. More effective accounts-receivable management relieved the tight cash flow.

The relationship between a firm's investment in receivables and its cash flow is summarized in:

FINANCIAL FACT

12

Accounts receivable
represent the primary source
of cash for a business.

A better cash flow develops whenever a business employs the dollars invested in its accounts receivable more efficiently. But a shorter average collection period may not offer the best approach to a higher return on a firm's total asset investment. A firm's credit and collection policies also affect its sales and earnings, and that makes accounts-receivable management a more complex task than it first appears. Chapter 9 discusses the major considerations that enter into that task.

9 Management Analysis: Accounts Receivable

The management analysis of a firm's investment in accounts receivable helps determine the appropriate credit and collection policies for a business. More liberal policies help boost sales and earnings but raise the cost of carrying the investment in accounts receivable. Alternatively, more restrictive policies dampen sales and earnings but help hold down the cost of carrying that investment. This chapter reviews the basic techniques for evaluating both. The appropriate credit and collection policies for a business will help boost the firm's ROI.

CREDIT TERMS

A business establishes credit terms to limit the length of time a customer can defer payment for an open-account purchase. Inevitably, some customers ignore or overlook that limit. But since prompt payment habits contribute toward the general estimate of a firm's creditworthiness, most customers pay within the terms set by suppliers. So credit terms exert a significant influence on the length of a firm's average collection period and the size of its investment in accounts receivable.

Credit terms also influence the size of a firm's sales volume. Longer terms help increase that volume; shorter terms discourage sales. Management should recognize how a firm's credit terms influence both its sales volume and the size of its investment in accounts receivable.

The experience of the Phoenix Company can be used to demonstrate the management analysis of credit terms. Phoenix operates in a highly competitive market; no company in that market enjoys a competitive advantage from product, price, or service differentials. However, the company can gain a competitive advantage by extending credit terms that exceed the industry's present thirty-day norm. Consequently, the firm's management explored the gains from that potential advantage.

The evaluation process began with a review of the relevant aspects of the Phoenix Company's present operations:

1. The firm currently generates a $90,000 average monthly sales volume.
2. All customers observe the established thirty-day credit terms; that leaves the company with a $90,000 investment in accounts receivable.
3. The total asset investment, including accounts receivable, averages $500,000.
4. Phoenix realizes a 5% net profit margin from its sales.

Market research indicates that a fifteen-day extension in the Phoenix Company's credit terms will attract $20,000 in additional sales, or a cumulative annual increase of $240,000. If the 5% net profit margin remains constant, the increase will push up the firm's annual earnings by $12,000. The research also indicates that each additional fifteen-day extension in credit terms will have the same incremental effects on the company's sales and earnings.

The additional sales attracted by the longer credit terms also will increase the company's investment in accounts receivable. And that increase will exceed the rise in the monthly sales volume, since the company must extend the longer credit terms to all customers, the old as well as the new. Thus the analysis of the benefits anticipated from the extended credit terms cannot stop at the bottom line of the income statement. The analysis should focus on the impact the longer credit terms will have on the average return from the company's total asset investment. Table 9-1 illustrates one approach to that analysis.

Note that a $75,000 increase in accounts receivable (and total assets) will accompany the $20,000 sales increase anticipated from forty-five-day credit terms. That expansion must occur since the firm's average collection period will match the longer credit terms. Extending the Phoenix Company's

Table 9-1. Credit Terms and ROI; the Phoenix Company

Credit Terms (days)	Monthly Sales	Investment in Accounts Receivable	Annual Earnings	Total Assets	Return on Investment (ROI)
30	$ 90,000	90,000	54,000	500,000	10.8%
45	110,000	165,000	66,000	575,000	11.5%
60	130,000	260,000	78,000	670,000	11.6%
75	150,000	375,000	90,000	785,000	11.5%
90	170,000	510,000	102,000	920,000	11.1%

credit terms to sixty days will push sales up to $130,000 and the investment in accounts receivable up to $260,000. The longer selling terms will allow the average sales dollar to remain in the form of an account receivable for two months.

Table 9–1 also provides a view of the annual earnings and ROI the Phoenix Company can expect from the alternative credit terms. As noted above, each incremental $240,000 annual sales increase produces a $12,000 hike in earnings. Standing alone, that criterion suggests that the Phoenix Company should extend the longest credit terms possible.

However, the ROI criterion actually provides a better perspective for management. Another look at Table 9–1 indicates that extending the forty-five-day credit terms will raise the Phoenix Company's ROI from 10.8% to 11.5%. The higher earnings from the incremental sales easily compensate for the burden imposed by the larger investment in accounts receivable.

Extending the Phoenix Company's credit terms to sixty days provides another boost in the firm's ROI to 11.6%. However, the analysis indicates that extending credit terms beyond the sixty-day limit actually will lead to a lower ROI for the business. Terms beyond that limit create an increase in receivables that overburden the benefits from the incremental earnings.

Thus the Phoenix Company should extend sixty-day credit terms, which provides the highest ROI. Of course, error exists in any such analysis, so from a practical perspective, the forty-five-day credit terms appear more appropriate.

The Phoenix Company's circumstances are simplified in Table 9–1 to help demonstrate the analytic approach. Note that some complicating factors place a tighter limit on the benefits a business can obtain from longer credit terms.

First, we presumed that all of the company's customers pay according to the stated credit terms. However, some will take longer to pay, and that will diminish the benefits projected from the longer credit terms.

Second, we assumed that the projected sales hikes would not affect any of the company's assets, other than the accounts receivable. Yet an increase in sales usually requires a proportionate increase in the size of a firm's investment in inventory. A rise in sales also may call for an increase in other assets, such as operating cash and prepaid expenses. So limiting the analysis to the expansion in accounts receivable overstates the benefits the business can expect from the longer selling terms.

Realistically, the sales attracted by the Phoenix Company's longer credit terms will come at the expense of the firm's competitors. Logically, those competitors will quickly match those offered by the Phoenix Company. That will leave the firm with the same sales volume, but with longer credit terms and a larger investment in accounts receivable. A temporary increase in the firm's ROI eventually may develop into a permanent reduction.

Finally, some of the new customers attracted by the Phoenix Company's longer credit terms will become additions to the firm's bad-debt expenses. The longer a customer has to pay for a product, the greater the probability that he will lose the capacity to pay.

Despite these qualifications, the major point demonstrated by the Phoenix Company's analysis can be emphasized in:

FINANCIAL FACT

13

A change in credit terms
can increase the return
a business earns from
its total asset investment.

Measuring the relationship between credit terms and ROI becomes more complex when those terms allow cash discounts when a customer pays earlier than necessary. So those terms also must be analyzed.

CASH DISCOUNTS

Many businesses set credit terms that authorize cash discounts in exchange for early customer payments. For example, 2% 10, net 30-day credit terms mean that a customer gains a 2% discount off the list price of his purchase if he remits payment within ten days. Otherwise, the seller expects full payment in thirty days.

Cash discounts presumably benefit both parties in the transaction: The buyer reduces his purchase costs when he takes the discount, and the seller enjoys a better cash flow and a lower investment in accounts receivable. However, before introducing discounts into your credit terms, you should recognize how such allowances affect your earnings and ROI.

Returning to the Phoenix Company, let's assume that the competitive environment precludes any increase in the firm's present $90,000 monthly sales volume. Instead, management explored the prospects for improving the company's ROI by adding discounts to the existing thirty-day credit terms.

Research shows that half of the firm's customers will take advantage of a 1% cash discount allowed in exchange for payment within ten days. However, every customer will take a 2% discount allowed for early payment. Table 9–2 demonstrates how those payment habits will affect the Phoenix Company's operating results. Naturally, any discounts a business allows shrinks its profit margin. So either of the proposed credit terms will reduce the company's earnings. But the businessman who focuses on ROI doesn't make the bottom line of the income statement his sole management concern. He can justify a lower earnings total if a concurrent reduction in assets creates a higher ROI.

For the Phoenix Company, the reduction in assets anticipated from the proposed credit terms isn't adequate to provide a higher ROI. In fact, the 1% 10, net 30-day credit terms will lower the firm's ROI from 10.8% to 10.3%. Moreover, allowing 2% discounts for payments in ten days will reduce the company's ROI to 7.4%. Based on the summary analysis in Table 9–2, the firm should maintain its existing net thirty-day credit terms without allowing any cash discounts for early payment.

Additional analysis *might* justify adding the 1% discount for early payment to the Phoenix Company's credit terms, if the cash released by the reduction in receivables can be reemployed in other assets that help increase the firm's earnings. In many circumstances, redeploying a firm's asset investment provides the key to a higher ROI. But that potential seldom is large enough to justify allowing 2% cash discounts for early payments.

Don't presume that the results of the analysis illustrated in Table 9–2

Table 9-2. Cash Discounts and ROI; the Phoenix Company

Credit Terms (days)	% Taking Discounts	Discounts Allowed (annual)	Net Earnings	Investment in Receivables	Total Assets	Return on Investment (ROI)
30	—	—	$54,000	90,000	500,000	10.8%
1% 10, net 30	50.0%	$ 5,400	48,600	60,000	470,000	10.3%
2% 10, net 30	100.0%	21,600	32,400	30,000	440,000	7.4%

will always preclude cash discounts from a firm's credit terms. While the analytic format doesn't change, the results may vary. Some businesses will find that allowing a reasonable discount for early customer payments, such as 1% or less, helps increase the average return from their assets.

A FINANCIAL VIEW OF TRADE DISCOUNTS

A 2% discount for early payment obviously would be irresistible to the Phoenix Company's customers. But only half of the same customers will take advantage of a 1% discount allowed for payments made ten days after a purchase. Yet both discounts reduce a firm's net purchase costs. Recognizing the financial view of cash discounts explains that apparent contradiction.

A foregone discount represents an interest charge a business pays for borrowed funds. So when an option exists, the decision to take or skip a cash discount should focus on the annualized cost of those funds. Figure 9–1 illustrates this premise with a look at a $1,000 purchase made on 2% 10, net 30-day credit terms.

During the first ten days of the credit period, the purchaser enjoys the free use of $980 in credit consideration—the amount of the net, discounted purchase price. However, if he fails to pay by the tenth day, he pays the full $1,000 list price for the purchase. We can view the $20 difference between the discounted and the full list price as an interest charge the purchaser pays for using the initial $980 in credit consideration for an additional twenty days. That twenty-day term marks the length of the financing period, presuming the purchaser observes the upper limit set by the seller's credit terms.

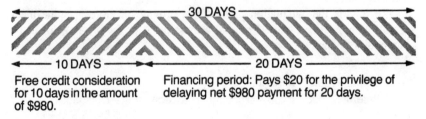

Free credit consideration for 10 days in the amount of $980.

Financing period: Pays $20 for the privilege of delaying net $980 payment for 20 days.

Fig. 9-1. A financial view of trade discounts. Assume a $1,000 purchase on 2% 10-day, net 30-day credit terms.

Of course, to complete the financial view, we should translate the cost of the foregone discount into an annualized interest rate. The cost of missing a $10 or $20 discount may not appear significant, yet many businessmen overlook the fact that such discounts represent the cost of the seller's credit consideration for a relatively short period of time. The proper management perspective develops only when that cost is annualized.

One approach to that perspective begins by determining the total number of financing periods that accumulate from a firm's credit terms during a standard 360-day business year. Referring to Figure 9–1, the seller's 20-day financing period occurs eighteen times over the course of a year ($360 \div 20$). The approximate, annualized interest rate appears when you multiply the number of credit periods in a year by the percentage cost of skipping a single discount.

For example, the business that foregoes a 1% discount allowed for payment in ten days pays an annualized 18% interest rate for the privilege of using the full 30-day credit period. Since that rate doesn't appear particularly high, it explains why only half of the Phoenix Company's customers will make the effort to take a 1% discount allowed for payment in ten days.

However, the same calculation process indicates that a business that foregoes a 2% discount pays a 36% annualized interest rate for the same credit consideration for the same term. Since almost every businessman will find that annual interest rate exorbitant, all customers would take advantage of a 2% discount.

The same calculation process can be used to determine the approximate annual interest rate a business incurs for missing any early-payment discount. Identify the number of credit terms within a year, then multiply that total by the percentage cost of each discount foregone. The final answer will not be precise, but it will indicate whether or not you should take a specific cash discount.

Reviewing the calculation process that provides a more accurate measure of the annualized interest rate a business pays for the privilege of using a supplier's financing:

$$\frac{\text{Annualized}}{\text{Interest Cost}} = \frac{\text{Discount Percent}}{(100 - \text{Discount Percent})} \times \frac{365}{(\text{Credit Limit} - \text{Discount Period})}$$

Using the 2% 10, net 30-day credit terms, we find:

$$\text{Annualized} \atop \text{Interest Cost} = \frac{2\%}{(100\% - 2\%)} \times \frac{365}{(30 - 10)}$$

$$= \frac{2\%}{98\%} \times \frac{365}{20} = \mathbf{37.2\%}$$

A business pays an annualized 37.2% interest rate whenever it misses a 2%, net 10 discount. The same formula will determine the cost of missing a discount included in any firm's credit terms. Table 9–3 lists the annualized percentage cost of missing the more common trade discounts.

Before missing a cash discount allowed for early payment, remember:

FINANCIAL FACT

To measure the cost
of missing a cash discount,
translate it into its
annualized interest rate.

A business can reduce the cost of missing a cash discount merely by delaying payment beyond the limit set by the seller's credit terms. For example, instead of paying for 20 days' credit consideration, or 2% 10, net 30-day terms, you could defer payment for another forty days beyond the

Table 9-3. Cost of Missing Cash Discounts

Credit Terms	Annualized Percentage Cost
1/10, net 30	18.4%
2/10, net 30	37.2
3/10, net 30	56.4
1/10, net 60	7.4
2/10, net 60	14.9
3/10, net 60	22.6

stated credit limit. The foregone discount then pays for sixty days in credit consideration. Delaying beyond the due date lowers the 37.2% annualized interest cost to 12.4%. (Use the formula above to confirm that reduction.) However, meeting the limits set by a supplier's credit terms remains a prudent management practice. The business that abuses a supplier's credit consideration risks losing it altogether. Certainly that risk is more severe than the cost of paying within the supplier's maximum term.

Also note that the cost a business incurs from allowing discounts matches the cost paid by the business that skips those discounts. The business allowing a discount for early payment actually pays the buyer interest (in the amount of the cash discount) for the privilege of obtaining payment for the purchase more rapidly. For both the buyer and the seller, the financial view of cash discounts for early payment should become an important management consideration.

CREDIT POLICIES

Although credit terms exert a significant influence on a firm's operating results, it is unrealistic to assume that every customer will pay within the limit set by those terms. Some pay late accidentally; others pay late deliberately. Still others pay late because they are unable to pay.

These unavoidable deviations mean that it is imperative to recognize the impact a firm's credit policies have on its operations. After all, those policies set the standards that qualify customers for credit consideration. They directly affect sales, earnings, and the size of a firm's investment in accounts receivable.

Conservative credit policies preclude sales to customers who can't demonstrate the financial ability and management intention to pay promptly. Such policies hold down a firm's investment in accounts receivable and reduce its expenses from bad-debt write-offs. But conservative credit policies also reduce a firm's sales and gross profits. Alternatively, liberal credit policies authorize sales to customers who clearly lack the ability to honor the firm's designated credit terms. That helps increase the sales and gross profits a business generates. But liberal credit policies also increase a firm's investment in accounts receivable and bad-debt expenses.

What is the relative influence more liberal or more conservative credit policies have on the return a business generates from its assets? Let's return to the Phoenix Company as an illustration. But now we will assume that the company is exploring the potential benefits that might accrue from relaxing its present strict credit standards.

Phoenix presently refuses sales to any prospective customer who lacks the ability to honor the firm's designated thirty-day credit terms. That makes the firm's bad-debt write-offs nominal, but it also restricts sales to the $90,000 monthly volume shown in Table 9–1. Logically, less restrictive credit standards should help increase the company's sales. And that increase should develop without the severe expansion in sales expected from longer credit terms. The new sales will lead to a higher investment in receivables. But the company's existing customers presumably will continue to honor the standard requirement for payment in thirty days. At the same time, a portion of the new sales approved under the loosened credit standards will become bad-debt write-offs. The Phoenix Company's analysis is summarized in Table 9–4.

First, Phoenix established a set of credit standards that separated its existing and prospective customers into four groups. The most creditworthy (Class A) customers clearly display the financial ability to honor the firm's specified 30-day credit terms. As noted above, that describes all of the company's existing customers. Competition precludes any additional sales to that customer pool. However, research suggests the following about the Phoenix Company's less creditworthy prospects:

1. Approving sales to Class B prospects will increase volume by $20,000 per month. On the average, Class B customers take 45 days to pay, while 2% of the sales to those customers will become bad-debt write-offs.
2. Another $20,000 monthly sales increase can develop from sales to Class C customers. However, those prospects take 60 days to pay, while 4% of the volume will remain uncollectible.
3. Sales to Class D customers can provide still another $20,000 monthly boost to volume. Those customers defer payment for 90 days and a startling 4% of the volume will develop into bad debts.

As shown in Table 9–4, the standard ROI criterion suggests that the Phoenix Company should loosen its standards sufficiently to qualify Class B customers for credit consideration. That will boost the firm's ROI from 10.8% to 11.5%. Of course, sales to Class C customers will further boost the firm's ROI to 11.6%. But that slight increment isn't sufficient to overcome the

Table 9-4. Credit Standards and ROI; the Phoenix Company

Customers' Credit Quality	Payment History (days)	Monthly Sales	Bad-debt Write-offs[a]	Investment in Accounts Receivable	Total Assets	Annual Earnings[b]	Return on Investment (ROI)
A	30	$ 90,000	—	$ 90,000	$500,000	$54,000	10.8%
B	45	110,000	$4,800 (2%)	120,000	530,000	61,200	11.5
C	60	130,000	7,200 (3%)	160,000	570,000	66,000	11.6
D	90	150,000	9,600 (4%)	220,000	630,000	68,400	10.8

[a] On incremental sales.
[b] Net of bad-debt write-offs.

margin of error inherent in the analysis. Extending credit to Class B customers marks the practical limit on the move to less restrictive credit policies for the Phoenix Company. In no event should the company approve sales to Class D customers. The increase in receivables and bad-debt write-offs anticipated from that category erases the benefit the boost in sales provides to the firm's bottom line.

The outcome of the Phoenix Company's analysis is less significant than the approach. Presuming the necessary data are on hand, the approach can orient the construction of a firm's credit policies. And the proper policies should contribute toward a higher return from the firm's assets.

INTEGRATED MANAGEMENT ANALYSIS

The discussion so far has segmented the management analysis of a firm's investment in accounts receivable. Realistically, you cannot focus on one segment while temporarily ignoring the others. All are closely interrelated and as such require *integrated* management analysis to recognize those interrelationships.

The Gilbert Electronics Company provides an example. Gilbert presently generates $1.2 million annually in sales on 2% 15, net 30-day credit terms. Presently, 75% of Gilbert's customers take the 2% discounts. Coupled with the nondiscount customer payment habits, that leaves the company with a 17-day average collection period and a $56,666 investment in accounts receivable.

Gilbert Electronics is considering changing its credit terms to 3% 10, net 45 days. Market research indicates that favorable customer response to the new terms will increase the firm's annual sales by $300,000. However, only 65% of Gilbert's customers will take the discount allowed for payment in ten days. The firm's average collection period will stretch to twenty days, and its investment in accounts receivable will rise to $75,000.

To justify the change, the proposed credit terms should increase the return from the company's assets. So some additional facts should be noted about the firm's circumstances:

1. Gilbert's present $1.2 million sales volume generates $60,000 in annual earnings
2. Those earnings represent a 15% return from the $400,000 average asset investment
3. Disregarding any change in cash discounts allowed, Gil-

bert will realize a 7% net profit margin from the new sales, or $21,000 ($300,000 × .07)

4. The sales increase will not have any affect on the asset investment, other than the change in receivables noted above

The first step in the integrated analysis determines how the proposed change in credit terms will affect the total cost of the cash discounts Gilbert Electronics allows for early payments:

Terms	Sales	% of Customers Taking Discounts	Total Cost of Discounts Allowed
3% 10, net 45	$1,500,000	65%	$29,250
2% 15, net 30	$1,200,000	75%	$18,000
Increase in Cost of Discounts Allowed:			$11,250

The new credit terms will increase the cost of the cash discounts Gilbert allows by $11,250 annually. That drops the contribution to earnings anticipated from the proposed change from $21,000 to $9,750. While that jump in earnings still appears significant, we cannot overlook the increase in assets that will accompany the new credit terms.

The only increase will appear in Gilbert Electronic's accounts receivable, which will increase from the present $56,666 level to $83,333. This will raise the firm's total asset investment to $426,667. Of course, the decision to implement the new credit terms hinges on the impact the change will have on Gilbert's ROI. So the total anticipated earnings must be related to the projected asset investment:

$$ROI = \frac{\$\ 69,750}{\$426,667} = \textbf{16.3\%}$$

The proposed credit terms will increase the average return from Gilbert's assets from 15% to 16.3%. The new credit terms will be beneficial for the business.

Although in different circumstances the analysis might produce different results, Gilbert Electronic's analysis helps illustrate the premise found in:

FINANCIAL FACT

Integrated management
analysis should precede
any change in a firm's
credit terms or policies.

Changing credit terms without an integrated analysis may actually lower a firm's ROI, even though the change appears promising measured by the firm's earnings.

10 Investment in Inventory

The need to have stock on hand to satisfy customer demand makes inventory a necessary asset, but a business should hold its investment in inventory to a minimum. This chapter reviews the fundamental formulas for analyzing the investment in inventory. Chapter 11 establishes the management perspectives that help increase the return a business earns from that investment.

FORMULAS FOR ANALYSIS

A sales forecast is the precedent for determining the proper size of a firm's investment in inventory. Presuming that a business begins with a realistic forecast, the components that make up that investment can be separated into three categories:

1. Sales stock
2. Safety stock
3. Expansion stock

Sales stock represents the foundation inventory a business needs to meet normal customer demand and satisfy anticipated sales requirements, perhaps measured by average daily or weekly customer purchases. Of course, customer demand seldom is completely predictable, and an average daily or weekly sales total obscures inevitable fluctuations in customer purchase habits. On some days, purchases fall below the norm registered by the average. On other days, they rise well above the average level.

These inevitable fluctuations require the addition of some safety stock to the inventory necessary to satisfy average daily sales requirements. Safety stock helps prevent the potential damage to customer relations and to future sales that can occur when a business lacks the inventory necessary to fill an order immediately.

The need for safety stock increases the total inventory, or total assets, a business needs to conduct its operations and naturally exerts a downward influence on the ROI. But so long as that safety stock doesn't become excessive, the ability to satisfy fluctuating customer demand should contribute to earnings and overcome that downward influence while enhancing the ROI.

Safety stock also helps protect a business against unforeseen disruptions in supplier shipments. Even the most reliable supplier can encounter a wildcat strike, a winter storm, or a production breakdown that delays deliveries. The business without an adequate safety stock will lose profitable sales in the interim.

Finally, in an effort to increase sales, a business should add some expansion stock to its inventory requirements. If the anticipated increase in sales fails to develop, the extra expansion stock will reduce the firm's ROI. But any business pressing for a higher sales volume must accept that risk.

Two calculations enable the management to analyze the investment in inventory:

1. Annual inventory turnover rate
2. Days' sales in inventory

The inventory-turnover-rate calculation measures how frequently a business recycles each dollar invested in its inventory during the year. More effective inventory management recycles each dollar more rapidly, reduces a firm's average investment in inventory, and increases its ROI.

Determining the days' sales held in a firm's inventory provides another, more useful perspective for management. It measures the average shelf life for the items that make up a firm's inventory. Reducing that term improves a firm's operating results.

THE ANNUAL INVENTORY TURNOVER RATE

An inventory item "turns" each time a business buys, sells, and, anticipating future sales, repurchases another copy for stock. The number of times that cycle recurs during the business year represents that product's annual turnover rate. Of course, practical management looks at the average annual turnover rate for all of the products included in inventory. Analysts traditionally determine that turnover rate as follows:

$$\frac{\text{Annual Inventory}}{\text{Turnover Rate}} = \frac{\text{Annual Sales}}{\substack{\text{Average Investment} \\ \text{in Inventory*}}}$$

*Or year-end investment in inventory

The annual inventory turnover rate for a business with $1,500,000 in sales and a $250,000 investment in inventory is:

$$\frac{\text{Annual Inventory}}{\text{Turnover Rate}} = \frac{\$1,500,000}{\$\ 250,000} = \mathbf{6}$$

The business turns the average item carried in its inventory six times during the course of the year. Of course, not every item in the firm's stock turns at the same rate. Some cycle more rapidly, while others have a slower turnover rate. But the overall average provides a logical starting point for positive inventory management.

Note that there is a flaw inherent in this calculation process. The sales total in the numerator includes the firm's gross profit margin—the markup over its product costs. So the calculation overstates the actual inventory turnover rate. A more accurate measure of a firm's inventory turnover rate can be obtained by using the cost-of-goods-sold total (CGS) as the numerator. For example, if the firm's cost of goods sold totaled $1,000,000 for the year, we find:

$$\frac{\text{Annual Inventory}}{\text{Turnover Rate}} = \frac{\text{CGS}}{\substack{\text{Investment in} \\ \text{Inventory}}} = \frac{\$1,000,000}{\$\ 250,000} = \mathbf{4}$$

The firm actually turned its inventory four times during the year. Using the sales total in the numerator adds two nonexistent turns to the annual inventory turnover rate. That addition overstates the firm's turnover rate by

Table 10-1. Annual Turnover Rate and Investment in Inventory

		Annual Cost of Goods Sold			
		$500,000	**1,000,000**	**2,000,000**	**4,000,000**
Annual	2	$250,000	500,000	1,000,000	2,000,000
Inventory	3	166,667	333,333	666,667	1,333,333
Turnover	4	125,000	250,000	500,000	1,000,000
Rate	5	100,000	200,000	400,000	800,000
	6	83,333	166,667	333,333	666,666
	7	71,428	142,857	285,714	571,428
	8	62,500	125,000	250,000	500,000

Investment in Inventory

50%. So using the cost-of-goods-sold total in the calculation provides a better measure for management.

Many popular sources of comparative financial data continue to use the sales total in the calculation process. Consequently, use the calculation consistent with that employed by your source of comparative data.

Table 10–1 offers a clear view of the direct relationship between a firm's annual inventory turnover rate and the size of its investment in inventory. It demonstrates that a more rapid turnover rate reduces the inventory level a business needs to conduct operations. For example, assume that a firm's annual cost of goods sold total $1,000,000. If the firm turns its inventory only twice during the year, it needs a $500,000 investment in inventory. Increasing the annual inventory turnover rate from two to three times a year lowers the inventory investment necessary to carry the same volume from $500,000 to $333,333. That frees almost $167,000 in cash for profitable reinvestment elsewhere. Another increase in the inventory turnover rate to four times a year lowers the necessary investment in inventory to $250,000 and frees cash that equals that investment.

A more rapid turnover rate translates into a smaller investment in inventory. Beginning with a target inventory turnover rate, use the following calculation to project the investment in inventory necessary to conduct any level of operations:

$$\text{Necessary Investment in Inventory} = \frac{\text{Projected Annual CGS}}{\text{Target Annual Inventory Turnover Rate}}$$

For example, a business projects a $1,200,000 annual cost of goods sold total and expects to turn its inventory four times during the year. The necessary investment in inventory becomes:

$$\text{Necessary Investment in Inventory} = \frac{\$1,200,000}{4} = \mathbf{\$300,000}$$

The calculation also helps identify the benefit a business can gain from a more rapid inventory turnover rate. Stepping up the above firm's annual turnover from four to five times a year lowers its required investment in inventory:

$$\text{Necessary Investment in Inventory} = \frac{\$1,200,000}{5} = \mathbf{\$240,000}$$

The more rapid inventory turnover rate lowers the necessary investment in inventory by $60,000. That reduction is a desirable management objective, since a business increases its ROI whenever it reduces the total assets necessary to conduct any level of operations. A firm's inventory turnover rate is an important management concern.

Recognizing the days' sales held in a firm's inventory makes a more direct contribution to the effort to control or reduce a firm's investment in that asset account.

DAYS' SALES IN INVENTORY*

Ideally, a business should begin each day with the minimum stock on hand necessary for that day's sales volume. This would eliminate any potential overinvestment in inventory. But few businesses can predict daily customer demand accurately, and few suppliers are able or willing to replenish a firm's

---

*Day's sales in inventory is analogous to the average age of a firm's inventory employed in Chapter 5.

exhausted stock daily. Most businesses carry inventory sufficient to meet anticipated customer demand for several days, weeks, or months.

The need to carry stock sufficient to accommodate fluctuating customer demand doesn't justify an excess investment in inventory. A business should carry sufficient inventory, but not too much. To help achieve that balance, management should focus on the number of days' sales that inventory represents. A two-step calculation identifies that total.

The first step determines the average daily cost of goods sold (CGS)—the inventory that enters into a firm's daily sales. Using the financial data from the previous section, the calculation proceeds:

$$\frac{\text{Average Daily}}{\text{CGS}} = \frac{\text{Annual CGS}}{360} = \frac{\$1,000,000}{360} = \$2,777$$

The second step relates that average daily cost-of-goods-sold total to the firm's investment in inventory:

$$\frac{\text{Days' Sales}}{\text{in Inventory}} = \frac{\dfrac{\text{Total Investment}}{\text{in Inventory}}}{\dfrac{\text{Average Daily}}{\text{CGS}}} = \frac{\$250,000}{\$\ 2,777} = \textbf{90 days}$$

The business carries an investment in inventory sufficient to satisfy its average daily sales requirements for 90 days.

Table 10–2 shows that the size of a firm's investment in inventory shrinks as it reduces the number of days' sales carried in stock. For example, assume that a business with a $1,000,000 annual cost of goods sold decides to carry stock sufficient for its normal sales requirements for 60 days, which means a $166,667 investment in inventory. However, the required investment will drop to $125,000 if management determines that stock for 45 days' sales is adequate to meet anticipated customer demand. Shrinking the required stock to a level sufficient for only 30 days' sales further reduces the required investment to $83,333.

Recognizing the number of days' sales in stock also provides the critical insight into a sensible inventory control or reduction program. A businessman easily can relate that number to the time required to order and receive (or produce) replacement stock. Thus the ability to replenish its stock rapidly shrinks the number of days' sales a business needs to maintain in inventory. Identifying the annual inventory turnover rate does not provide the

Table 10-2. Days' Sales and Investment in Inventory

		Annual Cost of Goods Sold			
		$500,000	**1,000,000**	**2,000,000**	**4,000,000**
Days'	30	$ 41,666	83,333	166,667	333,333
Sales	45	62,500	125,000	250,000	500,000
in	60	83,333	166,667	333,333	666,667
Inventory	75	104,166	208,333	416,667	833,333
	90	125,000	250,000	500,000	1,000,000
	120	166,667	333,333	666,667	1,333,333
	150	208,333	416,666	833,333	1,666,667

Total Investment in Inventory

same direct contribution to practical inventory management. Remember this in:

FINANCIAL FACT

⊨16⊨

Recognizing the days' sales
a firm's stock represents
provides the best perspective
for inventory management.

11 Management Analysis: Inventory

A balanced investment in inventory is essential for the business seeking the maximum return from its assets (ROI). However, achieving that balance can represent a formidable management challenge. A business must avoid an excess investment in inventory while still carrying stock sufficient to satisfy most customer purchase requirements. This chapter reviews the analytic techniques that contribute to effective inventory management and help improve the total return a business generates from its assets.

FORECASTING INVENTORY REQUIREMENTS

A sales forecast is the starting point for effective inventory management. Ideally, that forecast is based on a knowledgeable assessment of the projected economic environment and the anticipated influence that environment will have on a firm's market. Recognizing the constraints set by competition, a business then should forecast its annual unit sales volume and disperse it across operating periods, either weeks, months, or quarters.

Every sales forecast contains a margin of error because unpredictable fluctuations in customer demand are inevitable. But even a casual forecast provides some basis for controlling the investment in inventory. The business that proceeds without a sales forecast loses that control.

Figure 11-1 provides an idealized view of the contribution a sales fore-

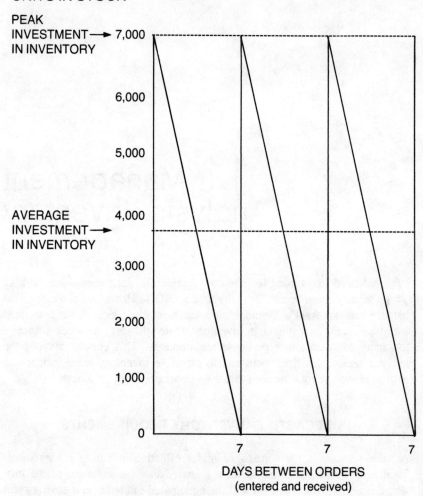

Fig. 11-1. Inventory control model. Days between orders assumes: 7,000 in weekly sales; 7,000 units is economic order quantity; 7-day order lead time.

cast makes toward controlling the investment in inventory. Beginning with the premise that the business carries only one product, the view develops from several additional assumptions:

1. An accurate sales forecast projects a 7,000-unit weekly volume for the business, or a 1,000-unit average daily sales volume
2. The economic ordering quantity for the business (identified by using the analysis in Chapter 12) is 7,000 units
3. Without fail, the firm's supplier makes delivery seven days after receiving each order

As shown in Figure 11-1, the business marks the beginning of each seven-day inventory turnover cycle as it receives a 7,000-unit shipment from its supplier, and it simultaneously enters a new order for that amount for delivery seven days later. At the instant received, each 7,000-unit shipment represents the firm's peak investment in inventory.

The business then sells the inventory at the steady 1,000-unit daily rate over the seven-day period, exhausting its stock immediately before the next shipment arrives from the supplier. The steady sales rate and dependable supplier delivery habit enables the business to meet its sales forecast with a 3,500-unit average investment in inventory. This represents the average of the peak 7,000 units on hand at the beginning of each cycle and the zero level reached at the end.

The *economic ordering quantity* (EOQ) sets the minimum possible investment in inventory for the business. However, an accurate sales forecast is the necessary precedent for identifying that quantity and achieving that ideal management objective. A business operating without a sales forecast can easily carry either too much or too little inventory. Either circumstance damages a firm's operating results. The critical contribution a sales forecast makes to the inventory control is emphasized in:

FINANCIAL FACT

17

A sales forecast is
a necessary precedent
for controlling a firm's
investment in inventory.

Of course, no business actually enjoys the balanced sales and supply circumstances of this theoretical firm. Businesses still need safety stock to meet unforeseen customer demands and occasional delays in supplier shipments. However, need for safety stock does not alter the basic approach to controlling a firm's investment in inventory. Instead, the need for safety stock merely increases the size of a firm's average investment in inventory.

Figure 11–2 illustrates this. Here we presume that the business recognizes the inevitable margin of error inherent in its sales and delivery forecasts. It also presumes that sales will never exceed the 9,000-unit level in any week. Nor will the firm's supplier ever be more than two days late delivering any order.

These presumptions make the 2,000-unit safety stock in Figure 11–2 a sensible investment for the business. The need for that safety stock raises the firm's average investment in inventory to 5,500 units—the 2,000-unit safety stock plus its 3,500 average sales stock. However, the basic approach to controlling the firm's investment in inventory remains the same.

ECONOMIC ORDERING QUANTITIES

Given the sales forecast, the economic ordering quantity for the same business actually determined the size of its average investment in inventory. But that does not represent the minimum possible investment. Without damaging sales, the business can further reduce the size of that investment by ordering smaller quantities more frequently. At the same time, the smallest possible investment in inventory is seldom the optimal level for a business. Instead, a business should balance the increase in costs from more frequent orders against the cost benefits that develop from carrying a lower investment in inventory. The economic ordering quantity for a product minimizes the

UNITS IN STOCK

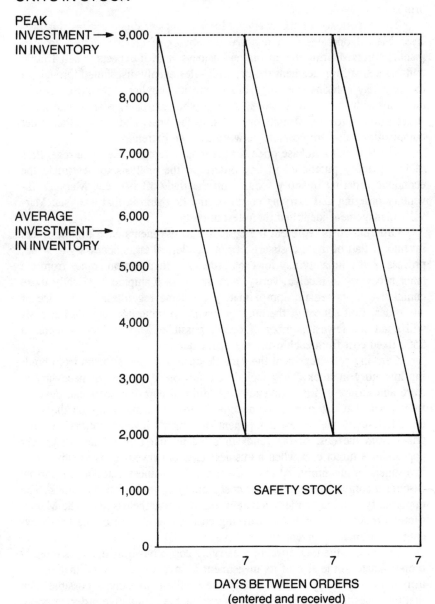

Fig. 11-2. Inventory control model with safety stock.

total of those two costs and also helps generate the highest return from a firm's assets.

The experience of the Marvel Motor Company demonstrates this process. Marvel operates as a regional distributor of electric motors to area manufacturers. During the upcoming business year, it expects to sell 16,000 units of a small replacement motor, with sales evenly distributed throughout the year. By entering one large order with its supplier, Marvell can begin the year with that total in stock. At the other extreme, Marvel can place sixteen orders for 1,000 units each during the year. Naturally, other order combinations also are possible between the two extremes.

The $10 unit purchase price for the motors remains the same regardless of the quantity purchased in any order. So the analysis to determine the economic ordering quantity focuses on the trade-off between Marvel's inventory ordering and carrying costs. As the first step in that analysis, Marvel's management identified the relevant costs.

Ordering costs represent the costs a business incurs each time it orders inventory. Part of those costs arise from the clerical tasks necessary to write, process, and ultimately pay for each order. Another portion comes from the labor necessary to receive, verify, and shelve each shipment. Usually those cumulative costs remain approximately the same regardless of the size of any order. Consequently, the business trying to minimize its ordering costs will enter the fewest number of orders possible. Marvel Motors incurs a $500 fixed cost from each order the firm enters.

Carrying costs represent the variable costs a business incurs from holding inventory in stock. They include the obvious expenditures necessary to store and ensure a firm's inventory. Additional carrying costs can develop from stock that deteriorates or becomes obsolete while it sits on the shelf unsold. Usually the largest component of a firm's inventory carrying costs arises from the cost of the funds invested in that asset. That component appears as a direct cost when a business uses borrowed funds to support its investment in inventory. At the same time, the business that doesn't borrow sustains a comparable opportunity cost from tying up its funds in stock. The opportunity cost may be less apparent, but it is nonetheless real. The Marvel Motor Company's cumulative carrying costs stand at 15% of the firm's average investment in inventory.

Of course, the total inventory carrying cost a business incurs is directly proportionate to the size of its investment in inventory. To hold that cost to a minimum, a business should carry the smallest investment possible. But that increases the number of orders as well as the cumulative ordering costs. Consequently, the economic ordering quantity for a product minimizes the combined total of the inventory carrying and ordering costs a business incurs.

Table 11-1 demonstrates how the Marvel Motor Company found the EOQ for its small replacement motors. First, management matched some alternative annual order frequencies with the order quantities necessary to fulfill the anticipated annual sales volume. Entering a single order for 16,000 units will hold Marvel's annual ordering cost to the $500 minimum amount possible. Smaller, more frequent orders naturally will increase the firm's annual ordering costs. Those costs will accumulate to the maximum total of $8,000 should the firm enter sixteen separate orders for 1,000 motors each.

Smaller, more frequent orders also will reduce the size of Marvel's average investment in inventory. To determine the averages employed in Table 11-1, Marvel's management employed the two simplifying assumptions introduced at the beginning of the chapter:

1. Sales occur evenly throughout the year
2. Each new shipment of replacement stock arrives at the instant the firm depletes its existing stock

Table 11-1. Determining EOQ; Marvel Motor Company

Number of Orders (1)	Order Quantity (units) (2)	Annual Order Cost[a] (3)	Average Unit Inventory[b] (4)	Average Dollar Investment[c] (5)	Annual Carrying Cost[d] (6)	Ordering Cost plus Carrying Cost (7)
1	16,000	$ 500	8,000	$80,000	$12,000	$12,500
2	8,000	1,000	4,000	40,000	6,000	7,000
4	4,000	2,000	2,000	20,000	3,000	5,000
8	2,000	4,000	1,000	10,000	1,500	5,500
16	1,000	8,000	500	5,000	750	8,750

[a] $500 per order
[b] (2) ÷ 2
[c] (4) × $10
[d] (5) × 15%

While both assumptions are unrealistic, they still provide a sensible foundation for management analysis. Given those assumptions, dividing any order quantity by two identifies the average investment in inventory that will develop from that quantity.

In Marvel's circumstance, the average investment in small motors will peak at 8,000 units—and $80,000—if the firm enters only one order for 16,000 units. Table 11–1 shows that the firm's annual carrying cost for that stock will total $12,000 ($80,000 × 15%). More frequent orders will reduce the firm's annual inventory carrying costs, reaching the $750 minimum should Marvel order 1,000 units sixteen times during the year.

The final step in EOQ analysis merely adds the ordering and carrying costs a business will incur from the alternative order quantities. The cost combination that minimizes that sum represents the economic ordering quantity for a product. Another glance at Table 11–1 indicates that the EOQ for Marvel's small replacement motors is 4,000 units. Either larger or smaller order quantities will raise the firm's total inventory above the $5,000 minimum that appears at that level. This point deserves emphasis in:

FINANCIAL FACT

The economic ordering
quantity (EOQ) for a
product minimizes a firm's
overall inventory costs.

A business should apply EOQ analysis to every product that represents a significant proportion of its sales.

At the same time, this approach to EOQ analysis can become tedious for the business that carries many products. Such a business will find the mathematical approach to EOQ analysis more appropriate.

THE MATHEMATICAL APPROACH TO EOQ ANALYSIS

The mathematical approach to EOQ analysis relies on a standard financial formula:

$$EOQ = \sqrt{\frac{2SO}{CP}}$$

S = anticipated annual unit sales
O = fixed costs per order
C = annual inventory carrying cost, expressed as a percentage of the product's purchase price
P = the unit purchase price for the product

Using the information from Marvel's analysis:

$$EOQ = \sqrt{\frac{2 \times 16,000 \times \$500}{(15\%)(\$10)}} = \sqrt{10,666,666} = \mathbf{3,266}$$

The economic ordering quantity for Marvel's small motors actually is 3,266 units. This falls well below the 4,000-unit total previously identified. However, using a 3,200-unit quantity and five total annual orders as an example, we can confirm the accuracy of the mathematical approach:

Annual Ordering Costs (5 × $500)	$2,500
Annual Carrying Costs ($32,000 ÷ 2 × 15%)	2,400
Total Inventory Cost	$4,900

Ordering 3,200 units five times a year will make Marvel Motor Company's inventory costs $100 less than the apparent $5,000 minimum identified above. This demonstrates the potential value of the mathematical approach to EOQ analysis. Indeed, its simplicity and accuracy makes it an indispensible inventory management tool.

Quantity Discounts in EOQ Analysis

Both illustrations of EOQ analysis held the product's price constant. However, many businesses offer a lower unit price when a customer makes larger quantity purchases. Such discounts can change a product's economic ordering quantity, so any potential quantity discounts should enter into the analysis that identifies the EOQ for a product.

Quantity discounts can be included in the mathematical approach to

EOQ analysis, but the necessary arithmetic adjustments are too complex to include here. Instead, we will see how quantity discounts enter into the approach to EOQ analysis introduced initially.

Assume that the price Marvel pays for its small motors depends upon the quantity purchased in any order. The unit price stands at $10.50 for order quantities of 1,000 or less. Then, as shown in Table 11–2, that price drops in twenty-five-cent increments as the alternative order quantities rise. Including all 16,000 motors in a single order will provide Marvel with a $9.50 minimum unit price.

The availability of quantity discounts does not alter the initial steps in EOQ analysis. The analysis begins by identifying the cumulative ordering and carrying cost a business will incur from alternative order quantities. After determining those costs, the analysis adds the additional expenses of *foregoing* any quantity discounts. The economic order quantity again becomes that which imposes the lowest total expenses on the business.

Here the quantity discounts raise Marvel's EOQ from 4,000 (or 3,200) units to 8,000 units. That ordering quantity will contribute toward higher earnings and a higher ROI.

Table 11-2. Quantity Discounts in EOQ Analysis;
Marvel Motor Company

Number of Orders (1)	Unit Order Quantity (2)	Price per Unit (3)	Quantity Discounts Foregone (4)	Ordering Cost plus Carrying Cost* (5)	Total Inventory Cost (6)
1	16,000	$ 9.50	—	$12,500	$12,500
2	8,000	9.75	$ 4,000	7,000	11,000
4	4,000	10.00	8,000	5,000	13,000
8	2,000	10.25	12,000	5,500	17,500
16	1,000	10.50	16,000	8,750	24,750

*From Table 11-1.

THE REORDER POINT

Determining the EOQ for a product remains a futile exercise unless a business determines the proper time to place an order. Assuming a constant sales rate, the reorder point is:

Reorder Point = Lead Time in Days × Daily Sales Rate

For example, assume that a business sells 5 units of a particular product daily. Also, it has to wait ten days for any order entered. As soon as the firm's inventory level (less safety stock) reaches 50 units, the firm should reorder an amount equal to the product's EOQ. Presumably the order will be received when the firm's sales stock drops to zero. The safety stock provides the inventory necessary to absorb an unforeseen jump in sales or delay in delivery.

Inventory Accounting and ROI

Effective control of a firm's investment in inventory helps increase the return from its assets. However, the inventory accounting method a business employs also influences its ROI. In an apparent contradiction, the inventory accounting method that produces a higher ROI may not be the best alternative for a business, as demonstrated shortly. Here let's establish a common perspective of the two major alternative inventory accounting methods, based on the experience of a small retailer, Autry Athletic Shirts.

Autry recently completed its first year in business. As an essential step in preparing the income statement for that year, Autry's accountant analyzed the store's inventory activity. Table 11–3 summarizes that analysis. Autry began operations with 1,500 athletic shirts in stock. The initial inventory cost $15,000, or an average of $10 per shirt. During the first six months in business, Autry purchased 6,000 shirts. However, the desire to upgrade the quality of the store's inventory, coupled with persistent inflation, drove the average price per shirt up to $12.

This trend continued during the second half of the year. Indeed, Autry's cost averaged $14 for the 6,000 shirts acquired during the last six months. The store closed its business year with 4,000 shirts remaining in stock. The accountant used the information in Table 11–3 to determine the value of the firm's year-end inventory. He measured that value using both of the major inventory accounting alternatives.

Table 11-3. Inventory Activity; Autry Athletic Shirts

	Shirts	Average Cost per Shirt	Total
Opening Day	1,500	$10.00	$ 15,000
Purchases, first six months	6,000	12.00	72,000
Purchases, second six months	6,000	14.00	84,000
Total Available for Sale	13,500	12.66	171,000
Ending Inventory	4,000	*	*

*Values depend upon accounting alternative selected.

First, he calculated the store's year-end inventory value using the *first-in, first-out* (FIFO) method of accounting. FIFO accounting proceeds on the logical assumption that a business sells its inventory in the order acquired. The first item purchased from a supplier presumably becomes the first product sold to a customer. At the end of the business year, the firm values its unsold inventory at the cost of the last items acquired. Applying this principle to the 4,000 shirts on hand at Autry's year-end, FIFO accounting calculated the value of that inventory:

$$4,000 \times \$14.00 = \$56,000$$

FIFO assumes that all of the unsold shirts on hand at the end of the year came from the 6,000 purchased during the last six months.

Second, the accountant measured the value of the same inventory using *last-in, first-out* (LIFO) accounting. LIFO proceeds on the premise that a business sells its inventory in reverse of the order actually acquired: The business sells its latest purchase before any like item previously held in stock. At the end of the year, the business values its unsold inventory at the oldest related costs. Applying LIFO inventory accounting to the 4,000 shirts Autry held in stock at year-end, the inventory value calculation becomes:

	Shirts		Cost Per Shirt		Total
(1)	1,500	×	$10.00	=	$15,000
(2)	2,500	×	$12.00	=	$30,000
(3)	4,000				$45,000

The LIFO calculation proceeds on the assumption that Autry's year-end inventory includes the store's opening day stock, plus the first 2,500 shirts out of the 6,000 purchased during the first six months of the year. Presumably, Autry sold none of these, but it sold all of the shirts purchased after the initial 4,000.

A two-step process illustrates how the two inventory valuation methods lead to a different measure of the return from Autry's total asset investment. The first step compares the effects the alternative inventory values have on Autry's cost-of-goods-sold calculation. This is a necessary preliminary to the calculation of Autry's earnings below.

Both cost-of-goods-sold calculations (Table 11–4) begin with Autry's $15,000 opening-day inventory. To that amount, both add the actual cost of the shirts acquired during the year. Note that either method leads to the same value for the store's total inventory available for sale. Then each alternative

Table 11-4. Comparative Cost-of-Goods-Sold Calculations; Autry Athletic Shirts

	FIFO	LIFO
Beginning Inventory	$ 15,000	$ 15,000
Purchases (actual cost) . . . . : . . .	156,000	156,000
Total Inventory Available (at cost)	$171,000	$171,000
Less: Ending Inventory	(56,000)	(45,000)
Cost of Goods Sold	$115,000	$126,000

subtracts the respective year-end inventory values to determine Autry's cost of goods sold. From the discussion, we know that LIFO leads to an $11,000 lower value for Autry's closing inventory than FIFO. Here that translates into an $11,000 higher cost of goods sold for the year.

Before we complete the second step in the illustration, we should emphasize an important point: Neither accounting alternative effects any material change in Autry's inventory. Indeed, the alternatives only lead to different accounting values for the same stock. That, in turn, affects the cost-of-goods sold calculation as illustrated in Table 11–4. Now, to complete the illustration, let's see how the different cost-of-goods-sold values influence the measure of Autry's ROI. Those values exert that influence through the earnings calculation summarized in Table 11–5. Note that FIFO accounting, with the lower cost-of-goods-sold total, leads to after-tax earnings $7,700 higher than those calculated with LIFO. Of course, higher earnings improve the return from a firm's asset investment. That holds true in this instance.

Before looking at the comparative ROI calculations, we should recognize another difference that develops from the alternative inventory accounting methods. Indeed, the lower ending inventory total produced by LIFO accounting affects a firm's balance sheet as well as its income statement. As that total reduces a firm's apparent earnings, it also shrinks its apparent asset investment. But that shrinkage seldom is sufficient to offset the depressing impact LIFO inventory accounting has on a firm's reported operating results.

For example, assume that FIFO inventory accounting left Autry Ath-

---

Table 11-5. Comparative Earnings Calculations;
Autry Athletic Shirts

	FIFO	LIFO
Sales	$230,000	$230,000
Cost of Goods Sold	(115,000)	(126,000)
Operating Expenses	(80,000)	(80,000)
Earnings Before Taxes (EBT)	$ 35,000	$ 24,000
Tax Obligation (at 30%)	(10,500)	(7,200)
Net Earnings	$ 24,500	$ 16,800

---

letic Shirts with $80,000 in assets—the $56,000 in inventory at actual cost plus $24,000 in other assets. LIFO accounting lowers that asset total to $69,000 because of the lower accounting value of the firm's inventory. Now we can compare the overall influence each accounting method has on the apparent return from the firm's assets:

	Net Earnings	Total Assets	Return on Assets (ROI)
FIFO Inventory Accounting	$24,500	$80,000	31%
LIFO Inventory Accounting	$16,800	$69,000	24%

Since it produces a higher ROI, the FIFO approach appears to be the more desirable inventory accounting method for Autry Athletic Shirts. However, another look at the comparative income statements above argues against that assessment. While FIFO accounting produces a higher ROI, it also allows the tax system to drain more cash from Autry. Indeed, without affecting the physical composition of Autry's assets, FIFO accounting produces a $3,300 higher income-tax obligation. The business that finds cash more advantageous than a higher ROI will select the LIFO accounting method for its inventory.

One more illustration, based on several assumptions, helps emphasize that fact:

1. Autry Athletic Shirts began operations with $25,000 in cash.
2. The store makes all sales for cash.
3. As a matter of policy, Autry pays cash for all purchases and operating expenses; the business defers no obligations in the form of accounts payable or accrued liabilities.

These assumptions help provide a clear view of the tangible cash benefit Autry gains from LIFO accounting. Table 11–6 provides that view with a look at the comparative cash flows that develop from the alternative inventory accounting methods. LIFO accounting leaves Autry Athletic Shirts with $11,800 cash at the end of the year—$3,300 more than that remaining should the business employ FIFO accounting. Autry must make a trade-off between the tangible benefit represented by additional cash and the management pride

Table 11-6. Comparative Cash Flows; Autry Athletic Shirts

	FIFO	LIFO
Beginning Cash	$ 25,000	$ 25,000
Add: Cash Sales	230,000	230,000
Less: Purchases	(156,000)	(156,000)
Operating Expenses	(80,000)	(80,000)
Taxes	(10,500)	(7,200)
Ending Cash	$ 8,500	$ 11,800

associated with a higher ROI. In this instance, Autry should accept the lower apparent ROI in exchange for the extra $3,300 in cash.

At the same time, in an inflationary environment, LIFO accounting actually provides a better perspective of the "real" ROI because higher inventory replacement costs absorb a portion of the apparent gains from sales. When prices are rising, FIFO accounting overstates the real ROI.

Consult an accountant before implementing any alternative accounting principles or procedures. But recognize the cash benefits that a business can gain from LIFO inventory accounting. Note that as volume expands and inflation accelerates, the cash benefits from LIFO accounting increase. Also recognize that any benefits from the original cash are enhanced by the warm glow any business manager feels when he reduces his income-tax obligation. That alone should compensate for the trauma associated with accepting a lower ROI.

SECTION FOUR
Structural Analysis

12 Liquidity in the Financial Structure

Few businesses grow and prosper without credit consideration, either in the form of trade credit from suppliers, direct cash loans from banks or other financial institutions, or even from employees who exchange labor for the company's promise to compensate them for that service on scheduled pay dates. Any credit consideration a business receives becomes a financial obligation. A business that fails to meet such obligations as agreed risks losing the opportunity to receive future consideration. That risk makes liquidity a major management concern.

Liquidity represents a firm's ability to meet its obligations on time, so it often determines a firm's creditworthiness. It also helps protect against the management trauma that develops when a business cannot meet its obligations on time.

Liquidity provides another form of financial protection: The more liquidity a business enjoys, the less likely a drop in sales, a strike, or some other business setback will lead to a financial crisis. Indeed, it provides a shield against financial failure, and even more liquidity strengthens that shield.

From another perspective, excess liquidity has a negative impact on the return from a firm's assets (ROI). Assets held primarily to improve a firm's liquidity seldom make a significant contribution to that return. The business must make a trade-off between the financial protection that comes from liquidity and a higher ROI.

This chapter demonstrates how liquidity enters into a firm's financial structure and influences the return from its assets.

A CONCEPTUAL VIEW OF LIQUIDITY

Because a business needs cash to meet its financial obligations, the cash balance is an important factor in any measure of liquidity. Ideally, from a creditor's viewpoint, a business should maintain cash on hand sufficient to pay all of its liabilities immediately. Of course, excess cash depresses a firm's ROI, just as any other asset overinvestment does. So a business should carry sufficient cash, but no excess. That raises the need to add some other assets to any measure of a firm's liquidity. Usually, that additional liquidity comes from a firm's investment in accounts receivable and inventory. As Figure 12–1 shows, it's easy to justify that addition since those assets revolve naturally through the cash flow cycle in a business.

Logically, the process begins with cash. Cash provides a business with the ability to purchase the inventory necessary for its operations, typically supplemented by trade credit consideration. The business then sells the inventory in exchange for accounts receivable from its customers. Collecting accounts receivable provides the cash the business needs to honor its obligations and continue the cycle. Of course, any disruption in the normal cash flow cycle reduces a firm's ability to meet its financial obligations promptly. A business cannot meet those obligations with uncollected accounts receivable or unsold inventory.

Even though the cash flow cycle revolves, there is an important distinction between the relative liquidity represented by accounts receivable and inventory. Both represent liquid assets, since a business usually can convert either into cash within a relatively short period. But accounts receivable contribute more toward any measure of a firm's liquidity than inventory. After all, predictable customer payments automatically convert receivables into cash. But converting any inventory into cash requires a sale. Then a business must wait to collect the receivable that actually proceeds from that sale.

The need to sell inventory or collect accounts receivable places natural limitations on the immediate contribution those assets make to a firm's liquidity. Nevertheless, that contribution is valuable to the business trying to improve the return from its assets. Indeed, a business should make the cash flow cycle function as efficiently as possible. A more efficient cash flow cycle enhances the return from a firm's assets.

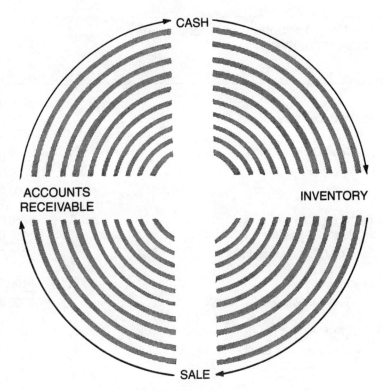

Fig. 12-1. The cash-flow cycle in a business.

A PRACTICAL VIEW OF LIQUIDITY

The comprehensive measures of a firm's liquidity focus on the relationship between current assets and current liabilities. The Cradle Company's 12/31/82 balance sheet in Table 12–1 helps illustrate why that relationship is an important management concern.

First, note that the Cradle Company's cumulative investment in current assets—cash, accounts receivable, and inventory—totals $600,000 on 12/31/82. That investment represents the firm's *gross working capital*. Since

Table 12-1. A Practical View of Liquidity; Cradle Company

Cash	$ 50,000
Accounts Receivable	250,000
Inventory	300,000
Total Current Assets	$600,000
Fixed Assets	200,000
Total Assets	$800,000
Accounts Payable	$250,000
Other Current Liabilities	150,000
Total Current Liabilities	$400,000
Long-term Debt	100,000
Total Liabilities	$500,000
Stockholder's Equity	300,000
Liabilities and Equity	$800,000

a firm's investment in current assets fluctuates directly in response to the prevailing level of its operations, that investment is viewed as "working" assets.

At any particular sales volume, the cash flow cycle in a business actually determines the total investment in gross working capital it needs to conduct a specific level of operations. Even the business that employs every dollar invested in its gross working capital as efficiently as possible must double that investment to handle a 100% increase in sales. Of course, the concern here centers on the liquidity represented by gross working capital. Calculating the firm's *net working capital* provides one estimate of that liquidity. Using the Cradle Company's financial circumstances, the calculation proceeds:

Gross working capital	$600,000
(Current liabilities)	(400,000)
Net working capital	$200,000

The Cradle Company's net working capital provides a $200,000 liquidity cushion for the firm's short-term creditors. That cushion comes from current assets provided by long-term lenders and stockholder's equity, rather than by short-term creditors. From another perspective, the Cradle Company's total assets can shrink by $200,000 before the business loses the ability to meet its current obligations by liquidating those assets.

What constitutes a reasonable level of working capital varies among businesses. The $200,000 level presumably appropriate for the Cradle Company may exceed or fall short of that appropriate for another business. Unfortunately, because of size and volume differentials, external comparison to the level of net working capital held by other firms is an unreliable management guideline. But introducing the basic working capital concepts here demonstrates the contribution liquidity makes to a firm's financial structure. That contribution is emphasized in:

FINANCIAL FACT

The liquidity in a firm's
financial structure enters
into any estimate
of its creditworthiness.

LIQUIDITY AND ROI

Cash, accounts receivable, and inventory represent a firm's investment in liquid assets, but accounts receivable and inventory are less liquid than cash. The cumulative investment in all three assets still contributes toward the general estimate of a firm's liquidity. The better that estimate, the more creditworthy a business appears.

Cash is a unique business asset. To provide the liquidity that actually preserves a firm's creditworthiness, it needs to invest in some cash "safety stock" to protect against unforeseen disruptions in its normal cash flow. Moreover, a business easily can justify an investment in cash that exceeds the level set by its normal operating and safety stock requirements. That justification develops when the business encounters spontaneous opportunities for profit that require immediate cash payment. Of course, the profitable opportunities must occur frequently enough to offset the downward influence the extra cash has on a firm's ROI. While that seldom poses a problem, let's look at the trade-off that should orient the decision to carry extra cash.

Assume that a business seeks a 15% average return from its assets. This objective then stands as the minimum standard, or the "hurdle" rate, for justifying any arbitrary addition to that investment. The business encounters occasional but unpredictable opportunities for profit that require cash in excess of the balance necessary for normal operations. Some opportunities come from cash-short suppliers who offer unexpected cash discounts in exchange for early payments. Others arise from distress sales that require cash payment at the time of purchase. Still others develop from the bargaining strength a business gains when it has the capacity to offer immediate cash payment.

Whatever the sources, the business can use the 15% return standard to help estimate the additional cash investment warranted by the normal, accumulated opportunities for spontaneous profits over the course of a year. An extra investment in cash makes sense when the anticipated contribution to the firm's incremental earnings represents no less than a 15% return on that investment. Table 12–2 demonstrates one approach that helps identify this beneficial "opportunity" cash.

The investment-return relationships illustrated in Table 12–2 reflect the logical progression associated with increases in a firm's investment in opportunity cash: The incremental contribution to earnings and ROI shrinks as the level of opportunity cash rises. Table 12–2 also demonstrates the contribution the ROI standard makes to financial management. Increasing the firm's opportunity cash from $80,000 to $100,000 leads to higher earnings, but a lower ROI on the asset. The business that ignores the ROI standard may invest in assets (cash included) that increase its earnings while depressing its ROI. That fact notwithstanding, a business can benefit from an investment in cash that exceeds the level determined by its normal operating requirements. This can be emphasized in:

Table 12-2. Opportunity Cash Analysis

Investment in Opportunity Cash	Anticipated Incremental Earnings	Return on Incremental Investment
$ 10,000	$ 5,000	50%
20,000	7,500	38
40,000	9,500	24
60,000	11,000	18
80,000	12,000	15
100,000	12,500	12

FINANCIAL FACT

A business often can
justify an apparent
overinvestment in cash.

Any apparent overinvestment in cash also enhances a firm's liquidity. The business becomes less susceptible to unforeseen setbacks that temporarily disrupt its normal cash flow cycle. That protection can make extra cash a wise investment, apart from the justification provided by potential opportunities for additional profits.

THE COSTS OF INADEQUATE LIQUIDITY

Effective liquidity management can boost the return a business generates from its assets. However, that potential should not encourage an overzealous management effort that presses the limit on a firm's minimum liquidity requirements. A management error that leaves a business with inadequate liquidity can be costly.

For example, inadequate liquidity can make a business miss cash discounts that suppliers allow for early payment for purchases. It also may spoil the potential for spontaneous profits that require cash. Or it can even force a business to pay high interest rates for the borrowed funds necessary to meet immediate requirements for cash. The potential costs of inadequate liquidity should stand as a prominent management concern in any business. Too much liquidity can damage a firm's ROI. But too little can threaten its survival.

13 Management Analysis: Liquidity

A business often can profit from an investment in liquidity that exceeds the level necessary to meet its predictable obligations. However, liquidity analysis focuses on the need to ensure that a business can meet all of its financial obligations promptly. That preserves the credit consideration essential for the success of every business enterprise. This chapter introduces the analytic tools that help identify the liquidity a business should have in its financial structure.

THE CURRENT RATIO

Liquidity analysis evaluates a firm's ability to meet its short-term financial commitments. The analysis focuses on the relationship between the current assets and current liabilities. The current ratio provides the most direct measure of that relationship:

$$\text{Current Ratio} = \frac{\text{Current Assets}}{\text{Current Liabilities}}$$

Using the Cradle Company's financial structure presented in Table 12–1 as the basis for illustration, the firm's current ratio at 12/31/82 is:

$$\text{Current Ratio} = \frac{\$600,000}{\$400,000} = \mathbf{1.5}$$

The current ratio indicates that the firm has liquid assets sufficient to meet its short-term obligations 1.5 times. That falls below the 2:0 current ratio that represents the traditional mark of an adequate level of liquidity for a business. However, without additional information, we can't draw a final conclusion about the adequacy of the Cradle Company's liquidity.

The liquidity necessary to make a business financially sound varies among different industries. The 1:0 current ratio generally acceptable for a transportation company is unacceptable for most manufacturers and wholesalers. The proper evaluation of any firm's current ratio requires a look at the comparative industry standard.

The predictability of a firm's cash flow also has a significant influence on the current ratio appropriate for operations. A business that enjoys a predictable cash flow can operate with a current ratio that appears low compared to the industry standard. Alternatively, a business that has to contend with an erratic cash flow needs extra liquidity—and a higher current ratio—to maintain the ability to meet its obligations promptly.

Another useful perspective for evaluating a firm's current ratio focuses on the shrinkage in current assets a business can absorb before it loses the ability to cover its current liabilities:

$$\text{Current Asset-Shrinkage Margin} = \left(1 - \frac{1}{\text{Current Ratio}}\right) 100\%$$

From the Cradle Company's financial structure, we find:

$$\text{Current Asset-Shrinkage Margin} = \left(1 - \frac{1}{1.5}\right) 100\% = \mathbf{33.3\%}$$

The Cradle Company's current assets can shrink by 33% before the firm will find it impossible to cover its current liabilities. The shrinkage margin appropriate for a business again varies with the circumstances, but a higher current ratio and a larger shrinkage margin provide additional protection for a firm's creditworthiness.

CURRENT RATIO VERSUS NET WORKING CAPITAL

Chapter 12 introduced net working capital as a measure of a firm's liquidity and noted that a business cannot use the net-working-capital totals registered by other firms as comparative criteria for liquidity analysis. A simple illustration clarifies that limitation and provides another view of the contribution the current ratio makes to the analysis of a firm's liquidity.

Assume that two companies have matching $100,000 net-working-capital totals. This suggests that the two companies enjoy a comparable level of liquidity. However, note that the equal net-working-capital totals come from the following current assets and current liabilities:

	Company A	Company B
Total Current Assets	$200,000	$1,000,000
Total Current Liabilities	(100,000)	(900,000)
Net Working Capital	$100,000	$ 100,000

The different magnitude of the two operations alters the presumption that the two businesses have a comparable level of liquidity. A look at the comparative current ratios for the two businesses makes that more apparent:

	Company A	Company B
Current Ratio	2:0	1:1

The comparative current ratios show that Company A enjoys a much higher level of liquidity. Since it accounts for the magnitude of an operation, the current ratio is the better indication of a firm's liquidity. At the same time, the ratio is the traditional indication of an adequate level of liquidity:

FINANCIAL FACT

A 2:1 current ratio represents the traditional mark of an adequate level of liquidity.

This traditional standard cannot be applied indiscriminately to every circumstance. Rather, the quick ratio is a more stringent criterion for evaluating a firm's liquidity.

THE QUICK RATIO

A business with a current ratio that appears satisfactory still may not have an adequate level of liquidity. This apparent contradiction develops when the composition of a firm's current assets or current liabilities become unbalanced. Another comparative view of two businesses illustrates this potential problem:

	Company X	Company Y
Cash	$ —	$ 7,500
Accounts Receivable	—	7,500
Inventory	20,000	5,000
Total Current Assets	$20,000	$20,000
Accounts Payable	$ —	$ 5,000
Notes Payable	10,000	3,000
Accrued Liabilities	—	2,000
Total Current Liabilities	$10,000	$10,000
Current Ratio	2.0	2.0

The current ratios suggest that both businesses are equally liquid. But the composition of each firm's current assets and current liabilities makes it apparent that Company Y has a much higher level of liquidity. Company Y's cash and accounts receivable provide a significant degree of liquidity compared to Company X's single, relatively illiquid current asset in the form of inventory. Moreover, Company Y's liabilities represent a comfortable distribution of obligations compared to Company X's single liability. Company X's 2:0 current ratio clearly does not represent an adequate level of liquidity.

Such contradictions mean that the current ratio should be supplemented with a more stringent test of a firm's liquidity. The quick, or acid-test, ratio fills that need. The quick ratio is similar to the current ratio except that it excludes inventory from the measure of a firm's liquid assets:

$$\text{Quick Ratio} = \frac{\text{Cash} + \text{Accounts Receivable*}}{\text{Current Liabilities}}$$

*Any marketable securities among a firm's current assets should be included in the numerator of the quick-ratio calculation.

Using the Cradle Company's financial position in Table 12–1 for illustration:

$$\text{Quick Ratio} = \frac{\$50,000 + \$250,000}{\$400,000} = .75$$

The contribution that the quick ratio makes to the management analysis of a firm's liquidity is self-evident. Inventory is generally a firm's least liquid current asset. By ignoring that asset, the quick ratio provides a better view of a firm's immediate ability to meet its obligations from cash and collections from customers. In fact, the liquidity implied by a high current ratio can disappear when a business also registers a low quick ratio. Industry norms provide a better measure of an acceptable quick ratio for a business, but recognize the traditional benchmark for evaluating a firm's quick ratio in:

FINANCIAL FACT

A 1:1 quick ratio represents the traditional mark of an adequate level of liquidity.

THE CASH RATIO

The cash ratio represents the most stringent test of a firm's liquidity. That ratio relates the firm's current cash balance to its current liabilities. In the Cradle Company's circumstance:

$$\text{Cash Ratio} = \frac{\text{Cash}^*}{\text{Current Liabilities}} = \frac{\$\ 50,000}{\$400,000} = .125$$

*Plus any marketable securities a business owns.

The Cradle Company has 12½ cents in cash on hand relative to each $1 in current obligations. Unfortunately, no reliable comparative standard exists for determining the appropriate cash ratio for a business. Indeed, the ratio that provides a business with sufficient liquidity depends upon the characteristics of its own cash flow. At the same time, the business that recognizes those characteristics can use the cash ratio as a supplemental tool for liquidity management. That ratio standard should be set high enough to absorb unforeseen disruptions in cash flow.

ASSET-ACTIVITY RATIOS

Complete management analysis of a firm's liquidity requires a look at the individual asset-activity ratios introduced in Section Three. After all, a 2:1 current ratio may reflect an excess investment in inventory rather than an adequate level of liquidity. Similarly, a quick ratio that meets the traditional standard for adequate liquidity may develop from an overinvestment in accounts receivable that leaves a business short of cash. Comparative analysis of a firm's asset-activity ratios helps clarify or contradict the implications raised by the traditional liquidity ratios.

From another perspective, effective asset management may enable a business to operate with liquidity ratios that fall below any comparative standards. Thus a business with an inventory turnover rate that exceeds the industry average can operate with a lower relative investment in inventory. The smaller investment in inventory will reduce the firm's current ratio without impairing its liquidity. At the same time, effective credit and collection policies may reduce a firm's average collection below the industry average. The smaller investment in accounts receivable that results from those policies also will lower the firm's quick ratio. However, the lower quick ratio reflects effective asset management rather than inadequate liquidity.

A hasty conclusion based on the traditional liquidity ratios easily can be incorrect. The management analysis of a firm's liquidity also should recognize how individual asset accounts affect that assessment.

14 Leverage in the Financial Structure

Financial leverage from borrowed funds magnifies the impact that any change in a firm's earnings has on the return on stockholders' equity (ROE). This chapter illustrates that financial phenomenon. Chapter 15 will review the management analysis that should precede any decision to employ financial leverage in a business.

A CONCEPTUAL VIEW OF LEVERAGE

Figure 14–1 helps illustrate how borrowed funds enter into a firm's financial structure and influence its operating results. Section A provides a conceptual view of the financial structure for a business that doesn't use any borrowed funds. Thus the stockholders' investment in the business is equal to its total assets. That makes the firm's balance sheet balance. However, the return on the stockholders' equity cannot exceed the return on assets. A 15% return on assets becomes a 15% return on the stockholders' equity. Remember that an increase or decrease in the ROI produces a matching increase or decrease in the ROE.

Section B in Figure 14–1 includes some borrowed funds in the firm's financial structure. We can presume that the business uses the borrowed

A. NO LEVERAGE

TOTAL ASSETS   STOCKHOLDERS' EQUITY

B. LEVERAGE

BORROWED FUNDS
TOTAL ASSETS   STOCKHOLDERS' EQUITY

Fig. 14-1. A conceptual view of leverage.

funds to replace a portion of the stockholders' equity, or more commonly, that borrowed funds are used as an alternative to raising additional equity from stockholders. This view is more appropriate, since the advantageous use of financial leverage magnifies the return stockholders' realize from any return on the firm's assets.

For example, assume that the financial structure represented by Section B in Figure 14–1 includes equal amounts of debt and equity: The structure contains $1 in debt for every $1 stockholders have invested in the business. This debt naturally imposes interest charges that exert a downward influence on the firm's ROI. However, the earnings from the incremental assets easily can exceed the additional interest cost. And here the financial leverage enables the business to employ $2 in assets to provide a return for each $1 in equity. This doubles the ultimate benefit that stockholders realize from the net return from the firm's assets. A 10% return from the firm's assets translates into a 20% return on the stockholders' equity. A 15% ROI becomes a 30% ROE. Indeed, the advantageous use of financial leverage magnifies the benefit stockholders gain from any particular return on a firm's assets.

Financial leverage exerts the same proportional influence on any loss that develops from a firm's operations. Thus the financial structure made up of equal amounts of debt and equity doubles the damage stockholders sustain from a firm's operating loss. An operating loss that represents a 5% reduction in a firm's assets, or a 5% negative ROI, translates into a 10% reduction in stockholders' equity. A 10% negative ROI becomes a 20% negative ROE.

Financial leverage magnifies the impact any firm's operating results have on the ultimate return (loss) those results represent for stockholders. A practical view of financial leverage will clarify that relationship.

A PRACTICAL VIEW OF LEVERAGE

A business with no financial leverage operates with an asset investment equal to the stockholders' equity. It produces a return on the stockholders' equity (ROE) that matches the return from its total asset investment (ROI). Naturally, any increase or decrease in the ROI will produce a corresponding increase or decrease in the ROE. However, a business can use financial leverage to increase its total asset investment well above the level supported by the stockholders' equity. Of course, stockholders enjoy the gain produced from all of a firm's assets, whether funded by debt or equity. So the advantageous use of leverage magnifies the return on stockholders' equity that develops from any ROI.

The experience of the Home Computer Company demonstrates that financial influence. Home Computer is a new venture poised for entry into the booming personal computer market. Enthusiastically supported by a group of entrepreneurial investors, the proposed venture has the following financial characteristics:

1. The business needs a $1,000,000 total asset investment to operate profitably

2. With those assets, the business will produce $250,000 in earnings during its first year in operation, excluding any potential interest expense
3. The investor group can fund the required assets with a $1,000,000 direct equity investment
4. Alternatively, the business can initiate operations with as little as $200,000 in stockholders' equity and borrow the funds necessary to finance up to $800,000 in additional assets
5. Any borrowed funds will carry a 15% annual interest charge

Using these characteristics as the basis for analysis, the investors focused on the return they could anticipate from four alternative financial structures for the Home Computer Company. Table 14–1 provides a comparative view of the four structures as well as a view of the net earnings, ROI, and ROE that would result from each alternative. It shows that Home Computer's first-year earnings and ROI will drop as the business increases the use of borrowed funds relative to equity. That drop isn't surprising since the firm's anticipated earnings before interest costs remain a constant $250,000, regardless of its financial structure.

Table 14-1. The Advantageous Use of Leverage;
Home Computer Company

| | Alternative Financial Structures | | | |
	1	2	3	4
Total Assets	$1,000,000	1,000,000	1,000,000	1,000,000
Total Liabilities (15% annual cost)	—	200,000	500,000	800,000
Stockholders' Equity	1,000,000	800,000	500,000	200,000
Earnings Before Interest Costs	250,000	250,000	250,000	250,000
Interest Cost	—	30,000	75,000	120,000
Net Earnings	$ 250,000	220,000	175,000	130,000
ROI	25.0%	22.0%	17.5%	13.0%
ROE	25.0%	27.5%	35.0%	65.0%

If Home Computer operates with $1,000,000 in equity and with no debt, it will produce $250,000 in earnings and a 25% ROI. At the other extreme, coupling $800,000 in debt with $200,000 in equity reduces the earnings from the venture to $130,000 and the ROI to 13%. Obviously, the difference in both instances arises from the $120,000 in interest charges that develop from that financial structure.

The drop in earnings and ROI induced by the interest costs suggests that borrowed funds are detrimental to the business. However, the comparative returns the investors can expect from the alternative financial structures contradict that assessment. In fact, as the investor group increases the use of borrowed funds, the return on each remaining equity dollar invested in the Home Computer Company rises. The financial structure with the minimum required $200,000 investment raises the anticipated return on stockholder's equity to 65%, which is well above the 25% ROE the investors can expect should they provide all of the funds necessary for the venture.

Presumably the investors seek the maximum possible return from their investments. So based on the analysis in Table 14–1, the Home Computer Company will initiate operations with the financial structure that requires the smallest equity investment ($200,000) and $800,000 in financial leverage. That frees the investors' other funds for other profitable uses.

Here it is more significant to recognize how leverage magnifies the return a firm's ROI ultimately represents for stockholders. As illustrated in Table 14–1, that financial phenomenon easily can offset the depressing impact interest charges have on a firm's earnings and ROI. But keep in mind that the benefits stockholders can realize from borrowed funds are not automatic. Financial leverage also magnifies the *negative* impact a firm's losses have on the stockholders' equity.

THE NEGATIVE EFFECTS OF LEVERAGE

The analysis has proceeded on the assumption that Home Computer Company's first-year operating profits will total $250,000. Of course, this total may vary. Competitive pressure, management error, or an uncertain economy can make a firm's earnings fall well below those originally anticipated. In fact, instead of operating profitably, a business may sustain a loss. Consequently, management also should recognize how financial leverage magnifies the impact an operating loss has on the stockholders' equity. Another look at the Home Computer Company illustrates that complementary analysis.

Table 14-2. The Disadvantageous Use of Leverage;
Home Computer Company

	Alternative Financial Structures (From Table 14-1)			
	1	2	3	4
Loss Before Interest Costs	($200,000)	(200,000)	(200,000)	(200,000)
Interest Costs	—	(30,000)	(75,000)	(120,000)
Net Loss	($200,000)	(230,000)	(275,000)	(320,000)
ROI	(20.0%)	(23.0%)	(27.5%)	(32.0%)
ROE	(20.0%)	(28.7%)	(55.0%)	(160.0%)

Assume that the investor group recognizes the potential for a maximum $200,000 first-year operating loss. Table 14–2 incorporates that prospect into the analytic format employed initially to illustrate the beneficial impact financial leverage has when a business operates profitably. But it also makes it apparent that financial leverage increases the damage stockholders' sustain when a business incurs an operating loss. And the more financial leverage a business employs, the more severe the damage becomes. The same financial structure that produces the largest return on equity from a successful business imposes the largest penalty when a business operates unprofitably. Whenever a business incurs an operating loss, financial leverage makes a bad situation worse. Remember this in:

FINANCIAL FACT

⊨23⊨
∨

Financial leverage
magnifies the return
on stockholders' equity
(ROE) that develops from
any return on assets (ROI).

THE EQUITY MULTIPLIER

The business that uses no borrowed funds operates with a total asset investment equal to the stockholders' equity. By using borrowed funds, a business can expand that investment and increase the scope of its operations. Consequently, we can view financial leverage as an *equity multiplier*. Financial leverage enables a business to multiply its total asset investment above the limit set by the stockholders' equity.

Financial leverage can be viewed as an equity multiplier from another perspective: Borrowed funds enable a business to increase the total assets it employs to earn a return for stockholders. Thus the business with the matching debt and equity totals has two dollars in assets working to provide a return for each equity dollar. Borrowed funds multiply the benefits any return on a firm's assets represent for each dollar committed by stockholders. In addition, that potential benefit can be measured directly. The first step identifies the specific equity multiplier at work in a business:

$$\text{Equity Multiplier} = \frac{\text{Total Assets}}{\text{Stockholders' Equity}}$$

To illustrate, the equity multiplier for a business with $300,000 in total assets and $100,000 in stockholders equity would be:

$$\text{Equity Multiplier} = \frac{\$300,000}{\$100,000} = 3$$

The business has three dollars working to provide a return for each dollar provided by stockholders. In other words, the business employs two dollars in borrowed funds relative to each dollar in equity.

If the business produces a 10% return on its total assets, the equity multiplier magnifies the return that performance provides to stockholders as follows:

$$\frac{\text{Return on}}{\text{Stockholders' Equity (ROE)}} = \frac{\text{Return on}}{\text{Assets (ROI)}} \times \frac{\text{Equity}}{\text{Multiplier}}$$

$$ROE = 10\% \times 3 = \textbf{30\%}$$

Since stockholders realize the net return from every asset dollar working for the business, the equity multiplier magnifies a 10% ROI into a 30% ROE.

Recognizing the equity multiplier in a business adds a new dimension to financial management. Holding its ROI constant, a business can increase the return on stockholders' equity by increasing its financial leverage and equity multiplier. It can provide a better return for its stockholders merely by increasing the use of borrowed funds. In fact, a high equity multiplier can transform an average earnings performance into an above-average return on the stockholders' equity.

There is another side to this view: A higher equity multiplier also magnifies the drain on stockholders' equity created by any operating loss. For the theoretical business, a 10% negative ROI will become a 30% negative ROE. It is important to recognize both perspectives of the new dimension that the equity multiplier adds to financial management.

FINANCIAL LIMITS ON LEVERAGE

The advantageous use of financial leverage benefits a firm's stockholders. The disadvantageous use of leverage penalizes the stockholders. Thus there are natural financial limits on the benefits a business can derive from using borrowed funds. Exceeding those limits will lower the return a business produces for its stockholders.

One view of the natural limits on financial leverage focuses on the interest charges and incremental operating profits (EBIT) a business anticipates from any borrowed funds. Logically, leverage becomes beneficial only when the incremental operating profits exceed the interest charges. This circumstance produces higher net earnings and, ultimately, a better return on the stockholders' equity. Leverage becomes disadvantageous for a business whenever interest charges exceed the incremental operating profits.

Another view of the financial limit on leverage develops from a comparison of the interest rate attached to any proposed debt to the operating return on a firm's assets. As noted in Chapter 7, the operating return on a firm's assets relates operating profits (EBIT) to total asset investment. For example, assume that a business produces $100,000 operating profits from a $600,000 total asset investment. The operating return from the firm's assets becomes:

$$\frac{\text{Operating Return}}{\text{on Investment}} = \frac{\text{Operating Profit (EBIT)}}{\text{Total Assets}} = \frac{\$100,000}{\$600,000} = \textbf{16.7\%}$$

Since it ignores any existing interest charges, the operating-return-on-investment calculation provides a pure measure of a firm's ability to produce a return from its assets. At the same time, that return marks the limit on the interest rate a business should pay for any borrowed funds, since the cost incurred from a higher rate will exceed the operating return produced from the firm's assets. The cost will exceed the benefit. To employ financial leverage beneficially, a firm must generate an operating return on its assets that exceed the cost of that leverage.

Management also should recognize another practical limit on financial leverage: The risk that naturally accompanies any leverage a business adds to its financial structure. This risk can erase the justification for using borrowed funds that appear beneficial when evaluated by the above criteria. Chapter 15 demonstrates how risk recognition enters into the management analysis of financial leverage.

15 Management Analysis: Leverage

The management analysis of financial leverage centers on three interrelated concerns. First, management should recognize the financial relationships that make leverage beneficial for a business. Second, since leverage magnifies the financial impact from an operating loss as well as the financial benefit from an operating profit, management should recognize the risk that accompanies any borrowed funds included in a firm's financial structure. Third, prudent leverage management ensures that a business presents a sound financial appearance for its creditors. A firm's liquidity affects that appearance, but too much financial leverage can discourage the approval of future credit consideration and hamper the growth and profitability of any business.

This chapter reviews the management analysis that helps determine the financial leverage a business can employ safely and beneficially while preserving its creditworthiness.

EVALUATING LEVERAGE RISK

Any decision to use borrowed funds should be based on the knowledge that leverage imposes the risk of larger losses as well as the potential for higher earnings. Also, the potential earnings should justify accepting the unavoidable risk of losses.

The Home Computer Company's circumstances illustrate one approach to evaluating that trade-off. But first let's clarify some implications from Chapter 14. Home Computer's circumstances were designed to emphasize how borrowed funds can magnify the return a business produces on its stockholders' equity. Naturally, that relationship also holds true for a business already in operation. But borrowed funds do not have to reduce a firm's earnings to produce a higher return on equity. Using them can simultaneously increase earnings and produce a higher ROE. Of course, the ROE drops whenever the cost of borrowed funds exceeds the incremental operating profits a business gains by using those funds. Remember, however, that a business seldom increases its financial leverage merely to finance its current level of operations. Instead, a significant increase in debt usually precedes—indeed, anticipates—a projected increase in sales.

The process follows a logical course. A business projects a larger sales volume, either from a planned expansion into new markets, the introduction of a new product, or merely from a more aggressive sales effort. As a necessary precedent to the projected sales increase, the business must expand its investment in fixed assets and inventory. Using borrowed funds to finance the necessary asset expansion naturally increases the firm's financial leverage—the amount of debt in its financial structure relative to the stockholders' equity. Should the business subsequently achieve the projected sales increase, the anticipated rise in operating profits presumably will pay the cost of the borrowed funds and increase the ROE.

However, the uncertainty inherent in futurity makes risk an inseparable companion of borrowed funds. A projected sales increase that triggers an increase in a firm's financial leverage may or may not actually develop. But the interest charges that arise from borrowed funds are certain, and they represent the penalty a business must pay when it fails to achieve any objective originally used to justify an increase in its financial leverage.

Leverage-risk analysis merely compares the projected benefits against the potential penalties that can develop from the different financial structures a business may employ. ROE represents the appropriate criterion for comparison. Table 15–1 illustrates that approach to comparative-risk analysis using the alternative ROEs developed for the Home Computer Company in Chapter 14.

The analysis begins with a comparison of the two extreme outcomes possible from the four alternative financial structures originally considered. An initial glance at that comparison merely reminds us of the basic relationship summarized in Financial Fact 23: Financial leverage magnifies the ROE

Table 15-1. One Approach to Financial Leverage-Risk Analysis; Home Computer Company

| | Alternative Financial Structures (From Table 14-1) | | | |
	1	2	3	4
Profitable Outcome	25.0%	27.5%	35.0%	65.0%
Unprofitable Outcome	(20.0%)	(28.7%)	(55.0%)	(160.0%)
Range	45.0%	56.2%	90.0%	225.0%

that develops from the ROI, whether the ROI represents the results of a profit or loss.

To gain a better comparative estimate of the risk associated with the four alternative financial structures, we must go a step farther and compare the ranges between the two extreme outcomes possible from each financial structure. Table 15–1 confirms that a larger range reflects a higher level of risk.

Excluding debt from Home Computer's financial structure will minimize the risk associated with the firm's projected operations. That financial structure holds the range between the best and worst possible outcomes down to 45%. As debt replaces larger portions of equity, the ranges between the two extreme outcomes increase. The maximum 225% range, the highest level of risk, develops from the financial structure that includes the maximum $800,000 in debt and $200,000 in equity.

Recognizing the risk that accompanies additional debt should encourage management prudence. A business should balance the higher return promised from additional financial leverage against the inherent risk. Unfortunately, the criteria for evaluating that trade-off are not well defined. What constitutes an acceptable level of risk in one circumstance may be inappropriate in another. Different business circumstances and different management dispositions create variations in the return necessary to justify any specific level of risk. In addition, few businesses enjoy the relative certainty implied in the Home Computer Company's circumstance—that is, an equal chance for either $250,000 in operating profits or $200,000 in operating losses. Usually, a business confronts a wide variation of potential outcomes, and that makes any assessment of the risk associated with a project more difficult, although the basic considerations that enter into the analysis remain the same.

The fact that any financial leverage-risk estimate is difficult only makes it more necessary. Even an uncertain risk assessment provides a better perspective for deciding whether or not a business should add leverage to its financial structure. The business that fails to make that assessment may face financial failure.

CREDITOR CONSIDERATIONS

The potential return a business can gain from additional financial leverage often justifies accepting the associated risk. However, risk acceptable to a particular business may be unacceptable to its creditors. From a creditor's viewpoint, excessive financial leverage raises doubts about a firm's ability to meet its debt obligations over the long run. Too many doubts can disqualify a business from further credit consideration. And the need to appear creditworthy may force a business to forego the return anticipated from additional financial leverage.

Several analytic tools can be employed to evaluate a firm's creditworthiness, and traditional standards set the limits on how much financial leverage a business can employ while still maintaining a creditworthy appearance. The business that observes those standards forfeits the potential return from higher levels of financial leverage. But the business that appears creditworthy also enjoys a sound financial condition that contributes toward its long-term survival.

The circumstances of the Happy Lamp Company illustrate the leverage analysis that qualifies a business for credit consideration. Table 15–2 provides a summary view of the relevant aspects of Happy's financial position and most recent year-end operating results.

The Leverage Ratio

The leverage (or debt) ratio measures the proportion of a firm's total asset investment financed by creditors. The higher a firm's leverage ratio, the more debt it employs relative to the stockholders' investment in the busi-

Table 15-2. Leverage Ratio; The Happy Lamp Company

Total Assets	$750,000
Total Liabilities	$500,000
(15% annual cost)	
Stockholders' Equity	$250,000
Liabilities and Equity	$750,000
Operating Profits (EBIT)	$125,000
Interest Charges	$ 75,000

ness, meaning the more financial leverage a firm has. A proportional relationship identifies the leverage ratio:

$$\text{Leverage Ratio} = \frac{\text{Total Liabilities}}{\text{Total Assets}}$$

Thus the Happy Company's leverage becomes:

$$\text{Leverage Ratio} = \frac{\$500,000}{\$750,000} = \textbf{66.6\%}$$

The Happy Company finances two-thirds of its total asset investment with borrowed funds. Creditors usually consider that proportion as the traditional limit on the financial leverage a business can employ safely. A higher leverage ratio increases the risk that existing or prospective creditors associate with a firm's operations.

The Debt-to-Equity Ratio

The debt-to-equity ratio relates the borrowed funds a business employs directly to the stockholders' investment. To find the debt-to-equity ratio for the Happy Company:

$$\text{Debt-to-Equity Ratio} = \frac{\text{Total Debt}}{\text{Total Equity}} = \frac{\$500,000}{\$250,000} = \textbf{2}$$

The Happy Company uses two dollars in borrowed funds compared to each dollar provided by stockholders, which corresponds to the usual two-thirds proportion, or 2:1 debt-to-equity, the traditional limit on the debt a business should employ relative to the stockholders' equity. A business with a higher ratio usually finds creditors reluctant to provide additional consideration. This limit on the financial leverage a business should employ deserves emphasis in:

FINANCIAL FACT

24

A 2:1 debt-to-equity ratio
marks the traditional limit
on the financial leverage a
business can safely employ.

This traditional limit is not necessarily appropriate for every business. Complete comparative analysis also must recognize the standard for the industry in which a business operates. But a debt-to-equity ratio that exceeds the traditional standard usually raises questions about a firm's creditworthiness. Holding the ratio below that limit implies that a business enjoys prudent financial management.

COVERAGE RATIOS

A satisfactory leverage or debt-to-equity ratio does not prove that a business has the ability to *service* its debts—that is, to meet its fixed obligations on time. Consequently, credit analysts complement the measures of a firm's financial leverage with a look at its *coverage ratios*. Coverage ratios relate a firm's operating results measured by its income statement to its fixed obligations. Those relationships provide essential estimates of a firm's ability to service its debt.

The Times-Interest-Earned Ratio

The times-interest-earned (TIE) ratio relates a firm's operating profits to the annual interest charges that arise from its debt obligations. A higher ratio adds more certainty to the estimate of the firm's ability to pay all interest charges as agreed. The Happy Company's data in Table 15–2, show the times-interest-earned ratio for the business as:

$$\text{Times Interest Earned} = \frac{\text{Earnings Before Interest and Taxes (EBIT)}}{\text{Annual Interest Charges}}$$

$$\text{Times Interest Earned} = \frac{\$125,000}{\$\ 75,000} = \mathbf{1.66}$$

The Happy Company produces operating profits sufficient to cover its interest obligations 1.66 times. Whether or not that provides an adequate coverage depends upon the stability of the company's operations. If sales and operating profits are relatively stable, the ratio might indicate adequate coverage. However, a larger ratio may be appropriate to offset the unpredictability associated with a firm's operations.

Creditors traditionally look for a larger margin of error than that provided by Happy's 1.66 TIE ratio. A ratio of at least 5.0 generally is deemed necessary to provide appropriate assurance that a business can meet its interest obligations. A business with that ratio can sustain an 80% drop in operating profits $[(5.0 - 1.0) \div 5.0]$ and still retain the ability to pay its interest charges.

The Fixed-Charge Ratio

Scheduled lease payments represent fixed obligations that a business must meet. The cumulative total of those obligations—lease payments plus interest charges—make up a firm's total annual fixed financial charges. The fixed-charge coverage ratio measures a firm's ability to pay those charges from the financial gains that develop from its operations. In that sense, the ratio is analogous to the TIE ratio. But lease payments represent business expenses already deducted from sales revenue in the process that identifies a firm's operating profits. Those payments enter into both the numerator and the denominator of the fixed-charge ratio calculation:

$$\frac{\text{Fixed-Charge}}{\text{Ratio}} = \frac{\text{EBIT} + \text{Lease Payments}}{\text{Interest Charges} + \text{Lease Payments}}$$

Assuming that the Happy Company has $40,000 in annual lease payment obligations, we find:

$$\frac{\text{Fixed-Charge}}{\text{Ratio}} = \frac{\$125,000 + \$40,000}{\$\ 75,000 + \$40,000} = \textbf{1.43}$$

The lease payments reduce the margin of error held in the Happy Company's operating results. The appropriate ratio will vary among businesses and industries, but creditors and lessors become more comfortable as a firm's fixed-charge ratio rises toward the 5.0 standard for the TIE ratio.

The Debt-Service Ratio

As emphasized in Financial Fact 6 in Chapter 4, net income plus depreciation measures the annual cash flow generated by a business. That measure becomes relevant here as an indication of a firm's ability to meet its fixed principal repayment obligations.

Principal repayments do not represent business expenses that flow through a firm's income statement. Instead, a business must generate an annual cash flow sufficient to make those repayments. Thus the relationship between annual cash flow and principal repayment obligations provides another measure of a firm's creditworthiness.

For example, assume that the Happy Company pays $10,000 in taxes on the firm's $50,000 in earnings after interest charges. That leaves the business with $40,000 in net income. Also, the business recognized $35,000 in depreciation expenses in its income statement and has $50,000 in fixed principal repayment obligations. We can find the firm's debt-service ratio as follows:

$$\text{Debt-Service Ratio} = \frac{\text{Annual Cash Flow*}}{\substack{\text{Scheduled} \\ \text{Principal Repayment}}} = \frac{\$75,000}{\$50,000} = \textbf{1.5}$$

*Net income plus depreciation.

The Happy Company's annual cash flow is sufficient to pay its principal repayment obligations 1.5 times.

The stability of a firm's annual cash flow naturally influences the debt-service ratio that it needs to appear financially sound. However, most businesses will need a 2.0 ratio to convince most creditors.

SECTION FIVE
Profit-Planning and Financial Forecasting Formulas

16 Profit-Planning Formulas

The unpredictability of the marketplace affects the success of every business enterprise, since it must contend with consumer whims, competitive pressures, and economic fluctuations. That uncertainty encourages many business managers to discard financial planning as a practical management tool because, presumably, an unpredictable future makes the planning effort futile. But financial planning actually represents the *best* response to an unpredictable business environment. It makes management aware of the interrelationships that determine a firm's operating results. That awareness enables management to respond to unforeseen developments that may pose a financial threat to the firm. Financial planning also can help a business improve its operating results and strengthen its financial position.

This chapter discusses the basic profit-planning process in a business. Chapter 17 complements that discussion with a look at the forecasting method that anticipates changes in a firm's financial structure. Together, the two chapters provide the management foundation a business needs to contend with an uncertain environment.

SALES VOLUME AND OPERATING RESULTS

A rise in profits usually accompanies an increase in sales. Moreover, in most businesses an increase in sales translates into a larger proportionate increase in profits. This financial phenomenon exists because a portion of the operating costs in most businesses are *fixed costs*, which remain constant regardless of fluctuations in a firm's sales. For example, fluctuating sales seldom have an immediate impact on a firm's salary, lease, depreciation, or administrative expenses. Over any particular operating period, those expenses remain the same whether sales rise or fall. This magnifies the change in earnings that develops from any change in sales.

To demonstrate the phenomenon, we also must recognize the other category of costs a business incurs, *variable costs*, which vary directly in proportion with sales. Thus a 50% increase in variable costs accompanies a 50% increase in sales. Product, packaging, and delivery costs are the more common costs that fluctuate in line with a firm's sales.

Recognizing the distinction between the two categories of a firm's costs, let's examine a business that presently carries only one product, which sells for $10. The business incurs $2,500 in monthly fixed operating costs and a $5 variable cost from each unit sold. A 50% increase in sales from 1,000 to 1,500 units per month pushes up the firm's operating profits:

Sales (units)	1,000	1,500
Sales (at $10 per unit)	$10,000	$15,000
Less: Variable Costs (at $5 per unit)	(5,000)	(7,500)
Less:	(2,500)	(2,500)
Operating Profits (EBIT)	$ 2,500	$ 5,000

A 50% rise in sales translates into a 100% increase in operating profits. The larger proportionate increase develops since the firm's fixed costs remained constant as sales jumped. Consequently, the full $5 difference between the sales price and variable cost from each incremental unit sold proceeds directly into earnings.

Finance professors define this relationship as *operating leverage*. The definition arises from the premise that fixed costs leverage any sales increase into a larger increase in operating profits. Obviously this relationship has some important implications for financial management. A firm's operating leverage increases as fixed operating costs become a larger proportion of total costs. This expands the boost in operating profits that a business gains from any increase in sales. For example, assume that prior to the 50% sales increase the firm had increased its monthly fixed operating costs from $2,500 to $4,000. This enabled it to reduce the variable cost incurred from each unit sold to $3.50. The increase in sales from 1,000 to 1,500 units per month then would have had the following impact on the firm's operating profits:

Sales (units)	1,000	1,500
Sales (at $10 per unit)	$10,000	$15,000
Less: Variable Costs (at $3.50 per unit)	(3,000)	(5,250)
Less: Fixed Costs	(4,000)	(4,000)
Operating Profits (EBIT)	$ 2,500	$ 5,750

The 50% rise in sales translates into a 130% jump in operating profits. The higher fixed costs provided the firm with a higher *degree of operating leverage* (DOL). As a general criterion, the following relationship defines the DOL in a business at any time:

$$DOL = \frac{\text{Percent Change in Operating Profit}}{\text{Percent Change in Unit Volume}}$$

Using the most recent example to illustrate, we find the firm's DOL as:

$$DOL = \frac{130\%}{50\%} = \mathbf{2.6}$$

With the $4,000 in fixed costs, that 2.6 DOL tells us that any increase in sales above the 1,000-unit volume will induce a 2.6-times larger increase in operating profits. Thus a 10% sales increase will boost operating profits by 26%. A 100% jump in sales will increase operating profits by 260%. The same proportionate operating leverage develops regardless of the size of the sales increase above the 1,000-unit level.

Conveniently, a firm's DOL can be measured without constructing the comparative income statements necessary for the calculation. This measure relates a firm's fixed costs to its current operating profits:

$$DOL \text{ at X Units} = 1 + \frac{\text{Fixed Costs}}{\begin{array}{c}\text{Operating Profits}\\ \text{at X Units}\end{array}}$$

Entering the data from above:

$$\text{DOL at 1,000 Units} = 1 + \frac{\$4,000}{\$2,500} = \mathbf{2.6}$$

This agrees with the DOL determined previously.

The opportunity to magnify the increase in profits that develops from any rise in sales suggests that a business always should employ a high degree of operating leverage. Presumably, fixed operating costs should represent a larger proportion of a firm's total costs at any sales level in order to enhance the gains realized from any subsequent rise in sales.

A high DOL often stands as a desirable management objective, but there is also a risk involved. As a high DOL multiplies the gains a business realizes from a sales increase, it also magnifies the financial damage that develops from any drop in sales. The circumstances of the same business helps illustrate that potential. But here let's assume that the firm's monthly sales volume drops from 1,000 to 500 units. The following comparison demonstrates how the 2.6 DOL magnifies the impact that 50% drop has on the firm's operating profits:

Sales (units)	1,000	500
Sales (at $10 per unit)	$10,000	$5,000
Less: Variable Costs (at $3.50 per unit)	(3,500)	(1,750)
Less: Fixed Costs	(4,000)	(4,000)
Operating Profits (EBIT)	$ 2,500	$ 750

The 50% decline in sales leads to a 130% decline in operating profits (50% × 2.6). Operating leverage exerts the same proportionate influence on the results that develop from a firm's sales fluctuations in either direction. Obviously, the business that seeks the gains available from a high DOL should not overlook the potential financial setback, since the more unpredictable a firm's sales volume, the more undesirable a high DOL becomes. That important relationship can be summarized in:

FINANCIAL FACT

◁25▷

Fixed operating costs
magnify the gains or losses
that develop from any
fluctuation in sales.

Note that interest charges from any debt a business employs are not included in the fixed-operating-cost total used to determine operating leverage. Operating leverage focuses on the impact a change in sales volume has on operating profits—earnings before interest and taxes (EBIT). Of course, financial leverage magnifies the impact any change in operating profits has on a firm's net earnings. A high level of financial leverage benefits any business that increases its operating profits, but it also increases the penalty any business sustains from a drop in those profits.

This relationship should be kept in mind when determining the degree of operating leverage to employ. A business with a high DOL should not simultaneously employ a high level of financial leverage. The combination makes the risk associated with a firm's operations too severe for a volatile economic environment. Alternatively, the business that functions with a low DOL often can accept a higher level of financial leverage. The lower risk associated with the DOL balances the higher risk associated with the financial leverage. These trade-offs should determine how much financial and operating leverage to employ.

BREAK-EVEN ANALYSIS

Fixed costs, both operating and financial, magnify the impact sales fluctuations have on a firm's operating results. At the same time, those costs usually are set as a business enters any particular operating period. Consequently, break-even analysis usually becomes the initial step in the profit-planning process for each period.

Break-even analysis identifies the minimum sales volume a business must generate in order to avoid sustaining a loss. When a business achieves that volume, total sales equal total expenses. The business neither makes nor loses any money. Break-even operating results are never satisfactory, but the analysis can help management maintain and improve operating results.

Break-even analysis proceeds from the same division of a firm's total costs into the usual fixed and variable categories. However, it includes a third critical element—the *contribution margin* that develops from a firm's sales. This margin represents the *difference* between the sales price and the variable cost of a product. For example, assume that a product that has an $8 per unit variable cost sells for $12. The contribution margin from each sale is $4, the sales price minus the variable cost. The contribution margin included in each sale helps pay a firm's fixed costs and ultimately provides any earnings the business generates.

Profit planning focuses on the accumulated contribution margin anticipated from a firm's total sales volume. Thus a business sustains a loss from its operations so long as the cumulative contribution margin from its sales remains insufficient to pay its fixed costs. Alternatively, a business breaks even at that volume where the accumulated contribution margin from its sales equals its fixed costs. Identifying that point provides the foundation for the profit-planning process. Finally, as a firm's sales rise above the break-even point, the incremental contribution margin proceeds directly to the bottom line. The business produces a profit.

Figure 16–1 helps to clarify the relationship between a firm's cumulative contribution margin. Figure 16–1 (a) represents the unit sales price of a company's only product. That price is divided into its two component parts—the variable cost and the contribution margin. The square in Figure 16–1 (a) represents the firm's total fixed costs, segmented into six equal units. Each subsection equals the contribution margin from a single unit sale of the firm's product.

Note the relationship between the contribution margin and the firm's operating results as sales are generated. Figure 16–1 (b) projects the results from a four-unit sales volume. The cumulative contribution margin from that volume isn't sufficient to cover the firm's total fixed costs. The business sustains a loss equivalent to the contribution margin held in one unit sale.

An increase in sales from five to six units eliminates that loss. As illustrated in Figure 16–1 (c), that sales volume generates a cumulative contribution margin equal to the firm's total fixed costs. Total revenue equals total expenses. The business breaks even.

Figure 16–1 (d) demonstrates the result of sales that exceed the break-even volume. An increase in the firm's volume to seven units creates earnings equivalent to the contribution margin from that incremental sale. The

Fig. 16-1. Break-even analysis: a conceptual view.

contribution margin from any additional sale also proceeds directly to the bottom line.

CALCULATING THE BREAK-EVEN POINT

The simplified circumstances of the Local Company demonstrate the calculations that identify a firm's break-even point. The Local Company carries only one product, which sells for $7 per unit, and it incurs $4 in variable cost from each unit sold. The contribution margin from each sale is $3. To break even, the company needs a cumulative contribution margin sufficient to cover the firm's $90,000 in fixed costs.

Given those facts, we can identify the Local Company's breakeven sales volume:

$$\frac{\text{Break-even Unit}}{\text{Sales Volume}} = \frac{\text{Fixed Costs}}{\text{Unit Contribution Margin}}$$

$$\frac{\text{Break-even Unit}}{\text{Sales Volume}} = \frac{\$90,000}{\$3} = \textbf{30,000 units}$$

A 30,000-unit or $210,000 total dollar sales volume (30,000 × $7) provides the cumulative contribution margin necessary for the Local Company to break even. Each sale in excess of 30,000 units provides $3 in profit. Should the company sell fewer than 30,000 units, the cumulative contribution margin will fall short of the amount necessary to cover fixed costs. That will create a loss equal to $3 for each unit the firm drops below the break-even sales volume.

Lower fixed costs can reduce a firm's break-even point. But obtaining a larger contribution margin from each unit sale achieves the same objective. Of course, a larger margin can develop only from a higher sales price or a reduction in the unit variable cost. The break-even calculation provides a perspective that can help management seek better operating results. Remember that in:

FINANCIAL FACT

26

Break-even analysis
provides the foundation
for profit planning
in a business.

Most businesses carry a number of different products, and the various products typically have different sales prices and variable costs and, consequently, different contribution margins. So practical break-even analysis often requires a different calculation process, although the critical concepts do not change. A look at the Able Axle Company helps illustrate that process. A summary of its income statement shows that Able Axle presently operates profitably:

Sales	$275,000
Variable Costs	(87,500)
Fixed Costs	(140,000)
Earnings	$ 47,500

Management anticipates a downturn in the industry that will reduce the firm's sales. Before initiating any defensive management actions, it wants to identify the firm's break-even sales volume. However, costs and sales prices vary widely among Able Axle's products, and no two products have the same contribution margin. So management cannot use the basic break-even calculation.

An alternative calculation, involving three steps, answers the same question, but it identifies the sales volume that produces a cumulative contribution margin sufficient to cover a firm's fixed costs.

Using Able Axle's income statement, the first step identifies the total contribution margin accumulated from all sales:

Total Contribution Margin = Total Sales − Total Variable Costs
Total Contribution Margin = $275,000−$87,500
Total Contribution Margin = **$187,500**

The second step determines the average contribution margin held in each sales dollar:

$$\frac{\text{Average Contribution}}{\text{Margin (per sales dollar)}} = \frac{\text{Total Contribution Margin}}{\text{Total Sales}}$$

$$\frac{\text{Average Contribution}}{\text{Margin (per sales dollar)}} = \frac{\$187,000}{\$275,000} = \textbf{68¢}$$

The contribution margin from the average Able Axle sales dollar is sixty-eight cents. That amount out of each sales dollar contributes toward Able's fixed costs and, after those costs are covered, its earnings.

The third step uses the average contribution margin figure to determine the break-even sales volume:

$$\text{Break-even Sales Volume} = \frac{\text{Fixed Costs}}{\text{Average Contribution Margin}}$$

$$\text{Break-even Sales Volume} = \frac{\$140,000}{.68} = \textbf{\$205,882}$$

The Able Axle Company can sustain a $69,000 drop in sales and still produce break-even operating results.

This alternative approach to calculating the break-even sales volume in a business is useful in any circumstance. The only prerequisite is the necessity to delineate between a firm's fixed and variable costs. But one important assumption qualifies the results of this calculation process: The proportional product mix that makes up any sales volume holds constant as that volume fluctuates. Even though the product mix in a firm's sales varies from day to day, changes in that mix seldom induce significant changes in the average contribution margin. The individual fluctuations tend to dampen one another. Consequently, the latter calculation process usually provides a reasonable management estimate of a firm's actual break-even point.

THE TARGET PROFIT SALES VOLUME

Since increasing profits from one operating period to the next remains an important measure of operating performance, a business often sets a predetermined level of earnings as an operating objective. With one alternation, the break-even calculation process identifies the sales volume necessary to achieve any target level of profits.

To demonstrate the calculation, let's assume that Able Axle's management wants to identify the sales volume necessary to generate $100,000 in earnings. The firm's fixed costs will remain constant, as will the average contribution margin held in each sales dollar. Management can use those facts to identify the sales volume necessary to produce the $100,000 target profit level:

$$\frac{\text{Target Profit}}{\text{Sales Volume}} = \frac{\text{Fixed Costs plus Target Profit}}{\text{Average Contribution Margin}}$$

$$\frac{\text{Target Profit}}{\text{Sales Volume}} = \frac{\$140,000 + \$100,000}{.68} = \mathbf{\$352{,}941}$$

Able Axle must increase its sales by $78,000 to generate $100,000 in earnings. A business that carries only one product can employ the same approach using the simpler calculation introduced initially.

The principles and procedures that enter into the profit-planning calculations are relatively simple, but they remain only exercises in arithmetic until you employ the concepts to improve your firm's operating results.

17 Financial Forecasting Formula

The profit planning formulas in Chapter 16 can help a business improve its operating results as measured by the income statement. But the financial impact from a firm's operations doesn't stop at the income statement. Those operations also exert a direct influence on the firm's financial structure—the balance sheet. For example, the business projecting a significant increase in sales usually must expand its investment in inventory in order to meet the anticipated rise in customer demand. Moreover, an expansion in the investment in accounts receivable and other assets typically accompanies any increase in sales.

Since a balance sheet must balance, an increase in liabilities or stockholder's equity must match any expansion in assets associated with a rising sales volume. This fact makes financial forecasting a positive management complement to profit planning. Neither the amount nor the source of the funds necessary to support any increase in assets should come as a surprise. From another perspective, the failure to foresee the need for those funds can threaten a firm's financial integrity. This chapter illustrates how the forecasting process can help a business anticipate its financing requirements.

Table 17-1. Video Electronics Company

	(8/31/82 FYE Balance Sheet)
Cash	$ 10,000
Accounts Receivable	125,000
Inventory	100,000
Other Assets	40,000
Total Assets	$275,000
Accounts Payable	$ 50,000
Other Liabilities	25,000
Total Liabilities	$ 75,000
Common Stock	$ 50,000
Retained Earnings	150,000
Liabilities and Equity	$275,000

THE DANGEROUS FINANCIAL GAP

To avoid financial gaps, the effective financial manager anticipates the impact his firm's operations will have on the financial structure. This is true even for the business that operates profitably. A look at the Video Electronics Company demonstrates this.

Video Electronics distributes electronic computer games to department stores in its area. Table 17–1 shows the firm's financial structure as it stood at 8/31/82:

1. A $2,500 average daily sales volume, coupled with a 50-day average collection period created the $125,000 investment in accounts receivable
2. The $100,000 investment in inventory and $10,000 in cash represent the minimum amounts necessary for the firm's present sales level
3. The $50,000 in accounts payable come from one month's purchases; all of Video's suppliers expect payment thirty days after purchase
4. Video Electronics earns $5,000 from each month's $75,000 sales volume

The mushrooming popularity of electronic games is pushing up the demand for Video's product line. In fact, market surveys indicate that the company easily can double its $75,000 monthly sales volume. Since Video's fixed costs will remain constant, the 100% increase in sales will produce a 200% increase in earnings. Specifically, the firm's earnings will jump from $5,000 to $15,000 per month.

Video decided to push for the higher sales volume. As the market surveys indicated, sales soon increased from $2,500 to $5,000 per day. Unfortunately, Video's management did not look past the operating results anticipated from the increase in sales. This shortsightedness opened the door to a severe financial problem. The natural expansion in assets from the higher sales volume created a large gap in the firm's financial structure.

Table 17–2 illustrates that gap with an imaginary view of Video's 11/30/82 balance sheet, three months after the decision to double the firm's sales volume. Look first at the asset section of the balance sheet. Since Video's operating characteristics remain constant, the increase in each asset account matches the 100% rise in monthly sales. The cumulative increase in assets totals $275,000.

Remember that the assets held in a firm's financial structure cannot increase independently. Video's liability and equity accounts must increase in some combination that matches and balances the $275,000 increase in assets. Note on Video's 11/30/82 balance sheet that a $75,000 increase in liabilities provided part of that necessary support. Accounts payable and other "spontaneous" liabilities typically fluctuate in line with a firm's sales. Here those liabilities doubled, matching the 100% jump in Video's sales rate.

Additional support for the higher asset investment came from Video's $45,000 in earnings ($15,000 per month) for the quarter ending 11/30/82. Since Video retained them, those earnings provided support for a matching amount of the increase in assets.

The cumulative increase in Video's liability and equity accounts ($120,000) falls far short of the $275,000 total necessary to make the firm's financial structure balance. Table 17–2 isolates the shortage as a $155,000 imaginary gap in Video's financial structure. The foresighted business fills any anticipated financial shortage with borrowed funds or additional investment by stockholders. Alternatively, the business that lacks foresight will sustain a cash shortage and an excessive increase in accounts payable that violates supplier terms for payment. To avoid such problems, management must forecast a firm's financing needs and prevent any unforeseen gap in the financial structure.

Table 17-2. Video Electronics Company

Cash	$ 20,000
Accounts Receivable	250,000
Inventory	200,000
Other Assets	80,000
Total Assets	$550,000
Accounts Payable	$100,000
Other Liabilities	50,000
Total Liabilities	$150,000
Common Stock	$ 50,000
Retained Earnings	195,000
Liabilities and Equity	$395,000
Financial Gap	$155,000
Total	$550,000

THE FINANCIAL FORECASTING PROCESS

The process that anticipates a firm's financing requirements proceeds through five straightforward steps:

1. Express any projected sales increase as a percentage of the current operating period's, such as the current year, quarter, or month.
2. Multiply the existing investment in current assets by the percentage sales increase anticipated during the upcoming operating period. This identifies the total asset expansion the business should expect.
3. Multiply accounts payable and accrued liabilities by the anticipated percentage increase in sales. This identifies the financial support for the asset expansion that will come from the spontaneous increase in liabilities.

4. Identify the increase in retained earnings expected during the upcoming operating period. This will equal the anticipated net earnings, less any dividend payments to stockholders.

5. Subtract the totals found in Steps 3 and 4 from that found in Step 2 to identify the net new financing requirements.

The Video Electronics Company's financial structure at its 8/31/83 fiscal year end (FYE) illustrates the financial forecasting process. As shown in Table 17–3, Video Electronics filled the $155,000 financial gap on 11/30/82 with a bank loan. The $15,000 in monthly earnings during the nine-month interim reduced that loan to the $20,000 residual amount remaining as a liability on 8/31/83. The firm expects to generate $2.7 million in sales during its fiscal year ending 8/31/84, which represents a 50% increase over the $1.8 million volume produced during the year ending 8/31/83. This expectation provides the basis for projecting Video's financing needs for 1984.

Multiplying the $550,000 in assets on 8/31/83 by 50% indicates that

---

Table 17-3. The Financial Forecasting Process; Video Electronics Company

	(8/31/83 FYE Balance Sheet)
Cash	$ 20,000
Accounts Receivable	250,000
Inventory	200,000
Other Assets	80,000
Total Assets	$550,000 × 50% = $275,000
Accounts Payable	$100,000 ⎱ × 50% = (75,000)
Accrued Liabilities	50,000 ⎰
Bank Loan	20,000
Total Liabilities	$170,000
Common Stock	$ 50,000
Retained Earnings	330,000 Net increase in = (125,000) retained earnings
Liabilities and Equity	$550,000
	Net New Financing Requirements = $ 75,000

Video should anticipate a $275,000 increase in its total asset investment during 1984. The business will need an increase in liabilities and stockholders' equity in any combination that matches that asset expansion. Table 17–3 shows that Video can expect a **$75,000** contribution toward the necessary financial support from the 50% expansion expected in its accounts payable and accrued liabilities. Presumbaly those liabilities will continue to expand spontaneously at the same rate as the firm's sales.

Video Electronics also expects to produce $250,000 in earnings from its $2.7 million sales volume in 1984. However, half of those earnings will flow out of the business as dividend payments to stockholders. Video will retain only $125,000 of its total earnings to help support its expected expansion in assets. Interrelating the above totals enables us to forecast Video's financing requirements for 1983 as shown in Table 17–3:

Anticipated Asset Expansion	$275,000
Less	
Anticipated Spontaneous	
Increase in Liabilities	(75,000)
Less	
Addition to Retained Earnings	(125,000)
Net New Financing Requirements	$ 75,000

Video needs $75,000 to maintain a balanced financial structure during the upcoming year. It may obtain the funds from an addition to its bank loan or perhaps from the sale of new equity.

Financial forecasting makes a critical contribution to a business by enabling management to foresee the need for new financing and avoid precipitating a financial crisis. The business gains time to arrange for the necessary financing or finds ways to reduce the need for financing. That contribution is apparent in:

FINANCIAL FACT

⊨27⊨

Financial forecasting
helps anticipate a firm's
financing requirements.

THE FINANCIAL FORECASTER'S PERSPECTIVE

Financial forecasting anticipates the asset growth associated with a projected increase in sales and then identifies the internal financial resources available to support the increase in assets. Should internal resources prove insufficient, the forecast measures the size of the potential gap in the firm's financial structure. A business can fill that gap with some form of external financing, either with additional debt or equity. However, external financing may not always be the best approach to filling a financial gap. Financial forecasting may indicate that no new financing is necessary.

For example, deferring the scheduled dividend payments will eliminate Video's need for new financing. Or management might implement more stringent credit standards to reduce the firm's average collection period. That will erase a portion of the increase in receivables anticipated from a projected rise in sales. Alternatively, a more effective inventory control effort might reduce the need for the additional inventory necessary to provide for the sales increase.

Financial forecasting offers a valuable perspective. The businessman who foresees the need for new financing gains the time to avoid a potential financial problem. He also is given another justification for employing the tenets of positive financial management.

18 Formulas for Financial Management

All of the formulas and ratios discussed throughout the book contribute to positive financial management. Some help increase the profits a business generates. Others help a business employ its assets more efficiently. Still others reduce the risk associated with operating a business. But those analytic tools cannot be applied randomly or as the need arises. Instead, the focal point for financial management centers on the return a business generates from its assets—its ROI.

Return on investment provides a standard for evaluating how efficiently management employs the average dollar invested in a firm's assets, whether that dollar came from stockholders or creditors. Moreover, a better ROI also translates directly into a higher return on the stockholders' equity. Focusing on ROI also provides the basis for integrating many of the management concerns that influence a firm's operating results. The manager who focuses on ROI gains an advantage in the competitive environment. This chapter presents a summary view of the beneficial management perspective that develops from using ROI as the focal point for financial management.

THE MANAGEMENT MODEL

Figure 18–1 shows the critical financial interrelationships that determine the return a business generates from its assets. To apply that view, you must use the calculation that identifies total asset turnover rate. A business that

Fig. 18-1. The ROI management model.

uses $400,000 in assets to generate $1,000,000 in sales determines its total asset turnover rate with the calculation:

$$\frac{\text{Total Asset}}{\text{Turnover Rate}} = \frac{\text{Sales}}{\text{Total Assets}} = \frac{\$1,000,000}{\$\ \ 400,000} = \textbf{2.5}$$

The business recycles the average dollar invested in its assets 2.5 times during the year. Analogous to the specific asset turnover rates in Section Three, the total asset turnover rate stands as another measure of management efficiency. As management employs a firm's assets more efficiently, the asset turnover rate naturally increases.

As shown in Figure 18–1, a firm's ROI results directly from the inter-relationship between net profit margin and total asset turnover rate. The ROI a business produces represents the product of that interrelationship: The total asset turnover rate multiplied by the net profit margin equals the return on investment. Assume that a business with $500,000 in total assets generates a $1,500,000 annual sales volume. A 5% net profit margin from those sales leaves the business with $75,000 in net earnings. Using the original ROI calculation:

$$\text{ROI} = \frac{\text{Net Earnings}}{\text{Total Assets}} = \frac{\$\ \ 75,000}{\$500,000} = \textbf{15\%}$$

However, a more useful perspective can be derived from the interrelationship presented in Figure 18–1:

$$\text{ROI} = \frac{\text{Net Profit}}{\text{Margin}} \times \frac{\text{Asset Turnover}}{\text{Rate}} = 5\% \times 3 = \textbf{15\%}$$

Both totals agree, but the calculation process as projected in Figure 18–1 makes it apparent that management can increase the ROI either by ex-panding its profit margin or employing its assets more efficiently. The business that may not be able to improve one element in the management model may do so in another.

THE NET PROFIT MARGIN

The net profit margin measures the average income a business extracts from each dollar in operating revenue. While total dollar profits remain important, the net profit margin indicates how efficiently a business operates. Better expense control creates a more efficient operation that produces a larger net profit margin.

Expressing each major expense category as a percentage of its total operating revenue is a useful approach for improving a firm's net profit margin. Figure 18–2 helps demonstrate that approach with a look at the operating results for a business that presently has a 5% net profit margin. That margin represents the remainder after subtracting trhe firm's operating and nonoperating expenses from its total revenue. Naturally, reducing the expenses in either category will expand the firm's net profit margin.

To provide a realistic estimate, the underlying expense accounts are expressed as a percentage of sales. The next level in the analysis separates the firm's total operating and nonoperating expenses into two categories each. Thus the product costs, the cost of goods sold, absorb 60% of the firm's operating revenue; selling and administrative expenses absorb another 20%. The firm's nonoperating expenses separate into interest charges equivalent to 10% of sales and taxes equivalent to 5%.

Even at this level, the potential benefits from this approach to analyzing net profit margin become apparent. First, the breakdown shows that the largest potential for improving the margin rests in the firm's cost-of-goods-sold account, the largest expense category. The effort to improve a firm's net profit margin logically should proceed in succession from the largest to smallest expense categories.

Figure 18–2 shows the beneficial impact a 10% reduction in the cost of goods sold—from 60% to 54% of sales—will have on the firm's net profit margin. The margin will increase dramatically from 5% to 11%. Of course, reducing any other expense category also will expand the net profit margin, but it will have a less dramatic impact.

Management's analysis of any cumulative expense total should proceed to each successive level of the elements that enter into that total. Thus the next level of the analysis of the firm's cost of goods sold might develop as shown in Figure 18–3. This breakdown provides a more precise look at the expenses that might be reduced.

The effort again proceeds in order from the largest to the smallest category of expenses included in the firm's total cost of goods sold, so here management should first explore the potential for reducing material costs. Any reduction in material costs will have the most significant impact on the firm's cost-of-goods-sold total and net profit margin. Management then should analyze the potential for reducing the other expenses included in the total cost of goods sold.

Logically, this analysis might look at the next level of underlying ex-

Fig. 18-2. The net profit margin in the ROI management model. All relationships are expressed as a percentage of the total operating revenue.

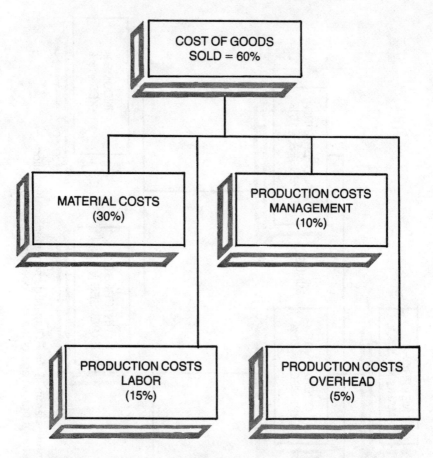

Fig. 18-3. Analyzing a firm's cost of goods sold.

penses included in each of the collective cost categories. Successive expense breakdowns may proceed through as many levels as make sense. In successive levels, this approach to analyzing a firm's net profit margin helps focus attention on the expenses that have the most significant impact on the firm's operating results. Any management action that reduces those expenses has the largest impact on the firm's net profit margin and ROI.

Holding the asset turnover rate constant, the following comparative relationships clarify the benefits of improving the net profit margin:

Asset Turnover Rate	× Net Profit Margin	= ROI
3.0	5.0%	15.0%
3.0	6.0%	18.0%
3.0	8.0%	24.0%
3.0	12.0%	36.0%

The results of improving the net profit margin can be emphasized in:

FINANCIAL FACT

Expanding the net
profit margin
increases a firm's ROI.

THE TOTAL ASSET TURNOVER RATE

The other element in the basic management model recognizes the influence effective asset management exerts on a firm's ROI. A business that cannot expand its profit margin still may increase its ROI by employing its assets more efficiently. More efficient asset management reduces the total asset investment a business needs to conduct any level of operations. Holding any profit margin constant, the increase in efficiency will improve a firm's ROI, as well as the return on stockholders' equity, the ROE.

To illustrate how to employ a firm's assets more efficiently, let's expand the basic ROI management model. Figure 18–4 shows that the total asset turnover rate develops from the interrelationship among the firm's individual asset accounts. Here we presume that the business has its $400,000 asset investment equally distributed among the four accounts, or $100,000 per account. Dividing the total investment into a $1,200,000 sales volume

Fig. 18-4. Development of a total asset turnover rate.

produces the firm's 3.0 total asset turnover rate. Presumably each individual asset account turns at the same rate.

Employing the dollars invested in any account more efficiently also increases the firm's total asset turnover rate. For example, assume that more effective inventory management enables the same business to reduce its investment in that asset from \$100,000 to \$75,000. This reduction increases the total asset turnover rate to 3.2 (\$1,200,000 ÷ \$375,000), as well as increasing the firm's ROI. To demonstrate, let's assume that the business extracts the maximum possible 5% profit margin from its sales. More efficient asset management affects a firm's ROI as follows:

Net Profit Margin ×	Asset Turnover Rate =	ROI
5.0%	3.0	15.0%
5.0%	3.2	16.0%
5.0%	3.6	18.0%
5.0%	4.0	20.0%

The initial increase in the firm's asset turnover rate increases its ROI from 15% to 16%. More rapid asset turnover rates push that return up further. This can be emphasized in:

FINANCIAL FACT

29

Increasing the total asset turnover rate increases a firm's ROI.

Improving a firm's inventory turnover rate requires analysis of the underlying assets included in the major account categories. For example, a better accounts-receivable turnover rate develops when a business presses slow-paying customers for more rapid payment. At the same time, recognize that even if a business has a satisfactory ROI, both analyses should be done, since a superior operating performance in one area can disguise a subpar performance in another. From a broad perspective, a business with a profit margin that exceeds the industry average may not be employing its assets as efficiently as possible. Alternatively, a higher asset turnover rate can obscure the potential for improving the net profit margin. The presumption that an acceptable ROI represents a satisfactory overall management performance will allow either deficiency to persist.

The same premise justifies the analysis of every successive level of the elements that determine a firm's net profit margin and total asset turnover rate. Specific operating expenses may be excessive even though a firm's net profit margin appears satisfactory. The assets held in a specific account may turn too slowly even though the firm's average asset turns at a satisfactory rate. Management should always proceed on the assumption that even a good performance always obscures the potential for improvement.

ROI AND ROE

Chapter 7 illustrates the relationship between the return on the asset investment (ROI) and return on stockholders' equity (ROE). A better ROI increases the ROE. Alternatively, any decline in ROI reduces the ROE. This relationship can be emphasized in:

FINANCIAL FACT

⊨30⊨

A firm's ROE fluctuates
in direct response
to any change in its ROI.

The changes will correspond exactly in the business that doesn't include any debt in its financial structure. After all, the stockholders' equity matches the firm's asset investment. The return on one account total must equal the return on the other. Of course, few businesses operate without the use of borrowed funds. Since those funds magnify the impact any change in ROI has on a firm's ROE, leverage should be added to our view of the basic ROI management model.

Adding Leverage to the ROI Management Model

The equity multiplier in Chapter 14 demonstrated the extent to which a business relies on both equity and borrowed funds to finance its assets. A business that employs one dollar in debt for every dollar in stockholders' equity has an equity multiplier of *two*. In other words, it has two dollars in assets working to provide a return for every dollar stockholders have invested in the business. This doubles the benefit stockholders realize from any positive

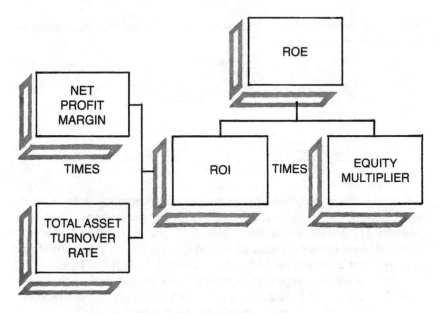

Fig. 18-5. Adding financial leverage to the ROI management model.

return from those assets, as well as the shrinkage in equity the stockholders incur from a negative ROI.

Any financial leverage magnifies the change in ROE that develops from any change in a firm's ROI. And the equity multiplier increases whenever a business expands the proportion leverage occupies in its financial structure. Figure 18–5 demonstrates how the equity multiplier enters into the ROI management model.

Note that the equity does not alter the basic relationship introduced at the beginning of the chapter. The ROI that a business generates still represents the product of the interrelationship between its net profit margin and total asset turnover rate. A better profit margin or a higher turnover rate improves a firm's ROI. Naturally, improvement in either area also produces a higher return for the stockholders' equity. However, Figure 18–5 makes it apparent that a higher equity multiplier also can improve the return stockholders realize from a firm's operations. We can summarize the cumulative financial interrelationships:

$$\frac{\text{Net}}{\text{Profit}} \times \frac{\text{Asset}}{\text{Turnover}} \times \frac{\text{Equity}}{\text{Multiplier}} = \text{ROE}$$
$$\text{Margin} \quad\quad \text{Rate}$$

or,

$$\frac{\text{Net Income}}{\text{Sales}} \times \frac{\text{Sales}}{\text{Total Assets}} \times \frac{\text{Total Assets}}{\text{Equity}} = \text{ROE}$$

The business introduced earlier demonstrates the complete financial interrelationship. That business produced a 5% net profit margin ($75,000) from its $1,500,000 annual sales volume. At the same time, it turned its $500,000 asset investment three times during the year. In the absence of any leverage, that translated the firm's profits into a 15% ROI and ROE.

Now we will assume that borrowed funds support half of the firm's asset investment. That makes the firm's equity multiplier two and produces the following impact on the return on the stockholders' equity:

Net Profit Margin		Asset Turnover Rate		Equity Multiplier		ROE
5%	×	3.0	×	2.0	=	30%

The equity multiplier in this instance doubled the benefit the stockholders gain from the firm's ROI. Indeed, a 15% ROI becomes a 30% ROE.

As the following comparison indicates, a higher equity multiplier increases the ROE that develops from any constant ROI:

ROI	× Equity Multiplier	= ROE
15.0%	1.0%	15.0%
15.0%	1.5%	22.5%
15.0%	2.0%	30.0%
15.0%	2.5%	37.5%

A high degree of financial leverage also can disguise an inadequate earnings performance or inefficient asset use. Indeed, a high equity multiplier can lead to an above average ROE even though a firm's actual operating results fall well below average. The business in such circumstances accepts an unnecessary level of financial risks.

At the same time, it is more important to recognize the valuable management perspective that develops when you add leverage to the ROI management model. You gain a clear view of all of the interrelated financial factors that influence the return a business produces for its stockholders—earnings, asset use, and financial leverage. And it becomes apparent that a poor management performance in any of the three areas will depress the financial return the business provides for its stockholders.

Recognizing how leverage affects the ROI management model completes the foundation necessary for an integrated approach to positive financial management. The business that employs this approach will increase its prospects for long-term financial success.

Glossary

ACCOUNTS PAYABLE. Amounts due for purchases made on credit.

ACCOUNTS RECEIVABLE. A claim against a debtor for merchandise sold or services rendered in exchange for the customer's promise to pay.

ACCOUNTS-RECEIVABLE TURNOVER. The net credit sales during a specific period divided by the average accounts receivable due from trade debtors; evaluates the quality of the accounts by relating the average total outstanding to the volume of credit sales.

ACCRUAL ACCOUNTING. An accounting method that recognizes sales when made and expenses when incurred, regardless of when the cash transactions actually occur.

ACQUISITION COST. The cost a business incurs from purchasing inventory, distinct from actual product costs, such as ordering costs.

ANNUAL CASH FLOW. The total of a firm's net income plus depreciation; the total measures the net incremental cash generated by operations over the course of a year.

ASSET TURNOVER. The ratio of total sales to total assets; a measure of the efficiency of asset utilization.

AVERAGE COLLECTION PERIOD. The average number of days each credit sales dollar remains outstanding; a qualitative indicator of the collectibility of a firm's accounts receivable.

AVERAGE CONTRIBUTION MARGIN. Total sales divided by total contribution margin.

AVERAGE INVESTMENT PERIOD. The length of time each dollar remains in inventory before a sale converts it into cash or accounts receivable.

BAD-DEBT WRITE-OFF. The loss incurred when an open-account sale proves to be uncollectible.

BALANCE SHEET. A financial statement that indicates what the firm owns and how those assets are financed in the form of liabilities and ownership interest.

BREAK-EVEN ANALYSIS. An analytic technique for studying the relationships among fixed costs, variable costs, and profits.

BREAK-EVEN CASH FLOW. The level of operations where total cash expenses equal total cash revenue.

BREAK-EVEN POINT. The volume of sales in a business where total costs equal total revenue.

CARRYING COSTS. Financial or operational expenses incurred from a firm's investment in assets.

CASH CAPABILITY. The total that comes from adding the firm's cash reserves to any available but unemployed credit consideration.

CASH CONVERSION PERIOD. The time lapse between the customer's decision to purchase a product and the date the payment for the purchase becomes cash available for reinvestment.

CASH FLOW CYCLE. The natural flow of cash through the operations in a business: cash to inventory to accounts receivable to cash.

CASH RATIO. Relates a firm's current cash balance to current liabilities; the most stringent test of liquidity.

COLLECTION PERIOD. See *Average Collection Period*.

COMMON-SIZE BALANCE SHEET. Expresses each account as a percentage of total assets or total liabilities and stockholders' equity.

COMMON-SIZE INCOME STATEMENT. Expresses each account as a percentage of total sales.

COMPONENT MANAGEMENT. The management effort that concentrates on control of the firm's investment in assets.

CONTRIBUTION MARGIN. Excess of sales price over variable expenses; an important element in break-even analysis.

COST OF GOODS SOLD. The cost associated with units sold during a specific time period.

COVERAGE RATIOS. Relates a firm's operating results measured by its income statement to its fixed obligations.

CREDIT POLICY. The guidelines used in the decision process that approves or disapproves of an open-account sale.

CURRENT RATIO. Current assets divided by current liabilities; a measure of a firm's liquidity.

DAYS' SALES IN INVENTORY. See *Average Investment Period*.

DEBT/EQUITY RATIO. The ratio of the total debt to the total equity employed in a business.

DEBT-SERVICE RATIO. Fixed principal repayments divided by annual cash flow (net income plus depreciation).

DEGREE OF OPERATING LEVERAGE (DOL). Percentage change in unit volume divided by percentage change in operating profits.

DEPRECIATION. A deduction of part of the cost of an asset from income each year of the asset's useful life.

EBIT. Earnings before interest and taxes.

EBT. Earnings before taxes; interest charges are deducted from operating profits.

ECONOMICAL ORDERING QUANTITY (EOQ). The optimum (least cost) quantity of inventory that should be ordered.

EQUITY. See *Stockholders' Equity*.

EXPANSION STOCK. Inventory added to help increase sales for the business seeking a higher sales volume.

FIFO ACCOUNTING. A system of writing off inventory into cost of goods sold; items purchased first are written off first; referred to as *first in, first out*.

FINANCIAL STRUCTURE. The firm's balance sheet.

FIXED ASSETS. Relatively permanent assets used in the operation of a business.

FIXED-ASSET TURNOVER. The result obtained by dividing the firm's sales volume by its investment in fixed assets; a measure of the efficiency in employing those assets.

FIXED-CHARGE RATIO. Measure the ability to pay annual fixed finance charges (lease payments and interest charges).

FIXED COSTS. Operating costs that remain constant regardless of the firm's sales volume; an important element in break-even analysis.

FYE. Fiscal year end.

GROSS PROFIT MARGIN. Total sales minus total cost of goods sold.

GROWTH STOCK. That portion of the firm's investment in inventory designed to satisfy an anticipated increase in sales.

GROSS WORKING CAPITAL. Cumulative investment in current assets—cash, accounts receivable, and inventory. Also called "working" assets.

INCOME STATEMENT. A financial statement that measures the profitability of the firm over a period of time; all expenses are subtracted from sales to arrive at net income.

INVENTORY. Goods, purchased or manufactured, held by a business for sale.

INVENTORY/SALES RATIO. The proportional relationship between a firm's investment in inventory and its monthly sales volume; a criterion for controlling the firm's investment in inventory.

INVENTORY TURNOVER RATE. The cost of goods sold for a period divided by the firm's average investment in inventory; a measure of inventory management efficiency.

INVESTMENT. The funds a business invests in accounts receivable, inventory, and fixed assets.

ITEM ANALYSIS. The technique that isolates the turnover rate associated with the specific items that make up the inventory in a business.

LEVERAGE. The ratio between the total debt and the total assets employed in a business.

LEVERAGE (OR DEBT) RATIO. Total assets divided by total liabilities. Measures the proportion of a firm's total asset investment financed by creditors.

LIFO ACCOUNTING. A system of writing off inventory into cost of goods sold; items purchased last are written off first; referred to as *last-in, first-out*.

LIQUIDITY. The ability of a business to meet obligations in a timely manner.

NET PROFIT MARGIN. Evaluates overall ability to squeeze profits from each sales dollar. Sales divided by net profits.

NET WORKING CAPITAL. Current liabilities subtracted from gross working capital; provides an estimate of a firm's liquidity.

NIFO ACCOUNTING. *Next in, first out* accounting for inventory, which uses inventory replacement costs to record the cost of goods sold.

OPEN-ACCOUNT SALE. A sale made in exchange for the purchaser's promise to pay on a later date; however, no promissory note is involved.

OPERATING LEVERAGE. Based on the premise that fixed costs leverage any sales increase into a larger increase in operating profits (EBT).

OPERATING PROFIT MARGIN. Deducting operating expenses (all costs incurred from normal operations, excluding interest charges and income taxes) from gross profits; the best measure of a firm's ability to make financial gains.

OPPORTUNITY CASH. Overinvesting in cash in order to increase earnings and enhance liquidity.

OPPORTUNITY COSTS. Earnings that might have been obtained if a productive asset, service, or capacity had been applied to some alternative use.

OVERINVESTMENT. Any cash committed to excess investment in accounts receivable, inventory, or fixed assets; or, extra assets unnecessary for the firm's level of operations.

PRETAX PROFIT MARGIN. Total sales divided by earnings before taxes (EBT); provides the best measure of actual earnings.

QUANTITY DISCOUNTS. Price reductions obtained by purchasing goods in larger lots.

QUICK RATIO. Similar to current ratio, but it excludes inventory from the measure of liquid assets.

RECEIVABLES/SALES RATIO. The proportional relationship between a firm's investment in accounts receivable and its monthly sales volume; a criterion for controlling the firm's investment in accounts receivable.

RETURN ON INVESTMENT (ROI). Earnings divided by average total assets; same as return on assets. A measure of the firm's operating efficiency.

RETURN ON STOCKHOLDERS' EQUITY (ROE). The yield that earnings represent relative to the accounting value of the stockholders' investment, or net profits divided by the stockholders' equity.

SAFETY STOCK. Inventory held by a firm in excess of anticipated requirements to protect against unforeseen shortages.

SALES/FIXED-ASSET RATIO. See *Fixed-Asset Turnover*.

SALES FORECAST. Projection of annual unit sales volume across operating periods, such as weeks, months, or quarters in order to control a firm's investment in inventory.

SELLING TERMS. The length of time a seller allows for payment of purchases made on credit; often includes discounts allowed for early payment.

STOCKHOLDERS' EQUITY. The total of common stock and all retained earnings.

STOCK-OUT COST. The opportunity cost that results from the inability to satisfy customer demand because of insufficient inventory; the firm loses the profit from a potential sale.

STRAIGHT-LINE DEPRECIATION. A method of depreciation that takes the depreciable cost of an asset and divides it by its useful life to determine the annual depreciation expense; straight-line depreciation creates a uniform expense every year an asset is depreciated.

STRUCTURAL MANAGEMENT. The management perspective that seeks to maintain the proper balance among the elements that make up the financial structure in a business.

TARGET PROFIT SALES VOLUME. The average contribution margin divided by fixed costs plus target profits.

TIMES-INTEREST-EARNED RATIO (TIE). Relates a firm's operation profits to the annual interest charges from its debt obligations.

TOTAL CONTRIBUTION MARGIN. Total sales minus total variable costs.

TRADE CREDIT. Interbusiness debt that arises from credit sales; recorded as an account receivable by the seller and as an account payable by the buyer.

TRADE DISCOUNT. A deduction in the list price of goods allowed by a seller in return for payment within a specified time; for example, 2% ten, net thirty-day terms allow a 2% discount from the list price if paid within ten days.

VARIABLE COST. A cost that is uniform per unit, but that fluctuates in total in direct proportion to changes in the related total activity or volume; an important element in break-even analysis.

Index